SECRETS OF THE HIDDEN JOB MARKET

Bob Rodgers
Steve Johnson
Bill Alexander
Edited by Phillip Schmitz

Betterway Publications, Inc.
White Hall, Virginia

Published by Betterway Publications, Inc.
White Hall, VA 22987

Cover design by Kay Chretien
Illustrations by Lee Jordan
Typography by EditSet

Library of Congress Cataloging-in-Publication Data

Rogers, Bob
    Secrets of the hidden job market.

    Bibliography: p.
    Includes Index
    1. Job hunting.   I. Johnson, Steve
II. Alexander, Bill   III. Schmitz, Philip.
IV. Title.
HF5382.7.R62   1986   650.1'4   86-18799
ISBN O-932620-62-0 (pbk.)

Printed in the United States of America
0987654321

Foreword

This book is dedicated to the idea that finding a job is a simple matter. Our job as authors is to try to make that idea easy to understand. In order to achieve this, we have attempted to make this book a straightforward, uncomplicated account of a job search.

As you will find, we have written in a way that is not difficult to understand. The words were carefully chosen for their brevity and meaning. But be aware that, although the approach is deceptively simple, the ideas are powerful tools which can help you again and again—if you put them into practice.

We hope that after reading this little book you will discover what we have learned.

Finding a job is a simple matter. If you know how!

The Authors

Contents

Introduction

This book is designed to point you in the right direction toward finding a job.

Although this book cannot actually *get* you a job, we are certain that you will find it extremely helpful and effective if you follow the steps we have outlined for exploring the job market.

This book will not make you want a job if you do not really want one in the first place.

It contains no magic.

If you are not willing to honestly examine your attitudes toward work, and if you cannot accept the fact that finding a job is a difficult task in itself, the odds are very much against your finding a job quickly.

If you can follow directions and if you really want a job *you can get one.* Bear in mind, however, that the job you get may not necessarily be the one you want. By the same token, the job you want may not necessarily be the one that you can get, at least for the moment. Smart people start thinking about their next job the minute they have landed their current one. It's like politicians who, once elected, immediately start thinking about running for a second term! (Think about it!)

◆ THE JOB MARKET DOES NOT EXIST. THERE IS NO ONE PLACE WHERE BUYERS AND SELLERS CAN GET TOGETHER.

Are a lot of people telling you that *there are no jobs due to high unemployment rates?*

Statements like this are among the most discouraging a job-seeker will hear. But do they really hold true? Let's examine matters more closely.

To say that the unemployment rate is 9% means that 9% of the available work force is out of work. On the other hand, it also means that 91% of the available work force is working!

It further implies that, since we have an ever-expanding population, there are more jobs available for more workers—every year!

In 1986 American businesses plan to create three million jobs, up from 2 million last year. The Dun & Bradstreet Corporation has predicted that nearly two-thirds of the new positions will be provided by small companies.

The annual Dun's 5,000 Survey said that companies in the finance, insurance and real estate fields are most likely to be planning to add employees this year.

If there are more jobs every year, and if we see no evidence of their existence, then we must assume that the jobs are somehow hidden.

◗ ACCORDING TO A U.S. DEPARTMENT OF LABOR STUDY, FOUR OUT OF FIVE JOBS FILLED EVERY DAY, EVERY WEEK, ARE NEVER ADVERTISED.

That same study found that of the jobs obtained, only 15% ever become visible at all. These 15% may be approached via the so-called "traditional" methods of getting work, i.e., the help-wanted ads, public employment agencies (State Job Service), private employment agencies, school or college placement services.

But what about the other 85% of the jobs?

Well, 48% of them were obtained through friends, relatives and acquaintances, through a process called *networking*.

The remaining 37% were found through direct contacts with employers. This means going *directly* to the employers and offering to work for them.

These two approaches add up to 85% and constitute the so-called "Hidden Job Market."

Let's return once again to that statement about the high unemployment rate being responsible for a lack of jobs. Is it beginning to look more like nonsense? It should, because even during the darkest days of the Depression, there were jobs. There are always jobs. If there happen to be fewer opportunities for work where you live, there may be only one solution: move. That's right! Even under the worst of economic conditions and in the tightest of economies, there are always jobs to be had.

Every day people die, resign, or retire, and they generally leave a job behind. New companies open for business, established companies expand or relocate. All this activity creates new jobs.

In order to take advantage of the Hidden Job Market you must recognize that the pattern of employment in any area is constantly shifting and changing.

What happens to the jobs held by people who retire, or resign, or die? They are certainly not just eliminated. Other people are moved up or over, transferred, shifted, entire departments are sometimes rearranged. But when all this activity comes to a halt, there still remain jobs to be filled.

Now, someone, be it the owner of the company or the personnel director, must make a decision about the vacancies. This decision, in turn, is based on the immediacy of the need. If matters are truly urgent, the decision-maker will place an ad in the newspaper, file a job order with the State Job Service, and may even contract the services of a private employment agency. (We are back to the 15% of all jobs which are accessible through the "traditional" methods.)

If, on the other hand, the need is not urgent, the decision-maker may rely on business associates, alumni, or anyone else who can recommend a candidate for the job. (This is often referred to as "The Old Boy Network." It contributes heavily to the 85%, the Hidden Job Market.)

Some employers do absolutely nothing until the right person walks through the door. In such cases we can speak of truly "hidden" jobs.

Here are ten steps you must take if you want to tap into the Hidden Job Market to find a job that's right for you:

- Face the facts—know the job market.
- Find out who you are—attitude is everything.
- Find out what you can do—assess your experience and abilities.
- Find out who does what you can do—check resources, do research.
- Prepare—résumés, applications, references.
- Prepare—practice interviewing, appearance.
- Start the job search—networking, approaching employ-employers.
- Follow-up—thank-you notes, calling back, etc.
- Evaluate your progress—if you are still not working, redo steps 1 through 8.
- Land (and keep) the job—now is the time for growth!

HOW PEOPLE GET JOBS

TRADITIONAL

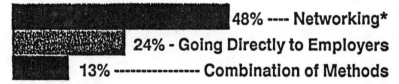

5% ----------------- Help Wanted ads

7% -------- School Placement

2% ------------------------------ State Job Service

1% --------------------- Private Employment Agency

15% TOTAL

HIDDEN JOB MARKET

48% ---- Networking*

24% - Going Directly to Employers

13% ---------------- Combination of Methods

85% TOTAL

* NET WORKING IS CONTACTING FRIENDS,
RELATIVES AND ACQUAINTANCES.

OR:

5	PEOPLE GOT THEIR JOBS THROUGH	:HELP WANTED ADS
7	" " " " "	:SCHOOL PLACEMENT
2	" " " " "	:STATE JOB SERVICE
1	" " " " "	:PRIVATE EMP. AGENCY
48	" " " " "	:NETWORKING
24	" " " " "	:DIRECTLY TO EMPLOYERS
13	" " " " "	:COMBINATION
100		

CHAPTER 1

The Importance of Your First Job

In his first job, a person often learns habits which last a lifetime. A person's attitudes about work, performance, and punctuality are established early in life. The force of habit plays a key role in daily life.

But we rarely think back to our first jobs. When we do, memory is likely to play tricks on us for we remember only a small part of what we have done or experienced. This makes it easy for us to underestimate the importance of those first experiences in the world of work.

What counts as a "first job"? Well, that decision is best made by the individual. We all have our own ways of deciding just when we "started to work," although there are some factors which apply to most of us. For example, was it a paid or an unpaid position? It might have been volunteer work for school, church, or some other social organization. It could have meant pitching in to make a family business run, or doing the chores at home.

As long as there was a schedule, a definite task to be accomplished, and a set of guidelines to perform the task, we can safely say that the person's activity did indeed count as work.

Such early work experience relates directly to peoples' present careers and the degree of satisfaction they are experiencing. When a person has job or employment-related problems, it is often necessary for an employment counselor to take a look back at the earlier stages of that person's vocational development. Sometimes we have watched people start entirely new careers and have had to wonder whether they were equal to the task. The success they later achieved demonstrated once again that habits and patterns can have a very positive effect. The person's first job might well have been a key factor.

We strongly advise our readers to review their own history of jobs and attitudes toward work when considering a career change or even a change of jobs within the same field. New beginnings often seem to hold so much promise that one is blinded to the real reasons for dissatisfaction with the previous job. Making a clean break should not prevent one's learning from past experience.

Know exactly where you're coming from before you decide to veer off in a new direction. In the retail field this process is called taking inventory. When your career is involved, it means that you should take a good hard look at skills and aptitudes that you have developed *over time*. The place to begin—you guessed it—is that very first job.

Examine your beginnings. Analyze your first job by breaking it down into its components. List the tasks it required, the skills you developed, and the goals you achieved. And be tough on yourself as you assess its contribution to your later occupational successes and failures. Make it a fearless inventory! Don't allow yourself the luxury of thinking it was ''just'' a job. Nothing could be farther from the truth.

While you are thinking about careers, jobs, objectives, skills, and the like, remember that you are not the only person doing this. Thousands of people just like you are thinking hard about improving their lives by improving their jobs. We would like to list some statistics that will give you some encouragement if the going gets really tough.

But first let us warn you about the *statistical trap*.* Numbers can be tricky!

If you are out of work, recognize that there are three sets of unemployment statistics: the national, the state, and the local unemployment rates.

> For example: National 7.5%
> State 8.3%
> Local 6.4%

---

*The concept of the ''statistical trap'' and the ideas that follow are taken from *The New Mosaic: Job Clubs*, by Bob Rogers, Steve Johnson, and Jack Crawford, Albany, NY: Beeline Books, 1985.

As you can see, the unemployment rate really depends on where you are. But what does this mean to you as a job-seeker? Being unemployed is a very personal situation. All of those numbers represent real people. Look at it this way. If you are employed, your unemployment rate is 0%; if you are unemployed, your unemployment rate is 100%.

Or try looking at it from another standpoint. If the national unemployment rate is 7.5%, then the employment rate is 92.5%. So, approximately eight people out of a hundred are not working, but 92 people out of a hundred are!

Remember that you are not just a number. You are not just another statistic. Don't fall into the statistical trap.

- The average time between jobs is 82 days—that's nearly 12 weeks.
- The best jobs do not necessarily, or even usually, go to the best qualified *people*. They are generally given to the best qualified *applicants*. This means that the people who know best how to market themselves are going to get the jobs.
- Most résumés are a waste of the job-seeker's time, money, and efforts, and will do virtually nothing to influence an employer positively.
- Most employers are rank amateurs when it comes to assessing, interviewing, or evaluating potential employees.
- The big difference between the person who has a job and the person who is looking for one . . . is that the first person knew how to find a job.
- Looking for a job is a job in itself, and one of the hardest you'll ever have, at that. The odds are that if you make a serious mistake on the job of finding a job, you won't be too happy with the job you get . . . and that you'll be out there looking soon again, and again, and again!
- The average worker *under* 35 goes job hunting about every 1½ years.
- The average worker *over* 35 goes job hunting about every 3 years.
- The average worker will change careers 3-5 times in his/her lifetime.

CHAPTER 2
Attitude

Our dictionary defines "attitude" as ". . . a mental position with regard to a fact or state." For the purposes of this chapter "attitude" can be defined as how a person feels about working.

In Chapter 1 we mentioned that a person's attitude toward work is very important. Getting a job requires willingness on the part of the job-seeker to do some very hard work. Your attitude toward work itself can be a significant factor in determining whether you are even capable of finding work.

If you dislike the idea of working, you need to take some time to examine the reasons why you feel this way. Have you had bad experiences with work in the past? Are there some jobs you would like, but can't get? Does work interfere with your spending time in other, more desirable ways? All of these things are at least partially true for most of us.

The other factor you must consider is that we must all find ways to meet our needs. For most of us, that personal satisfaction entails some form of regular work. Once we realize that we *must* work (there are very few "workable" alternatives), it's really foolish to go on fighting the idea.

▶ MY FATHER TAUGHT ME TO WORK, BUT NOT TO LOVE IT. I NEVER DID LIKE TO WORK, AND I DON'T DENY IT. I'D RATHER READ, TELL STORIES, CRACK JOKES, TALK, LAUGH — ANYTHING BUT WORK.

A. LINCOLN

The other day, we were talking with Dale Ellis, the director of a local service organization. His secretary had recently left on short notice and he had been interviewing applicants for the position. (All of them had been referred by people he knew.) He was desperate for someone with good steno, typing, and organizational skills, and several of the applicants had them. One had worked for a vice-president at the Xerox Corporation. Another had been secretary to the District Marketing Manager at General Motors. A third had spent 15 years with the regional office of the telephone company.

"I was a little overwhelmed by all this high-powered talent," Dale told us. "These ladies had all the qualifications I was looking for and then some. They were so efficient I could almost hear them clicking. Still, I decided to talk with one more applicant. Her name was Betty and she could only type 35 words per minute, and she couldn't take dictation very fast either. But, you know, she seemed really interested in the work I'm doing. She was so cheerful and encouraging that we got to talking and I told her all about our various programs and she thought they were great. By the time I finished chatting with her, I felt as if she had already been working for me for six weeks. What could I do but hire her?"

Notice the words Dale used when describing the women he *didn't* hire: high-powered, efficient. But how did he describe the one he *did* hire? Interested, cheerful, encouraging. Get the picture?

Employers don't hire machines, they hire people.

And which people do employers hire? People who are cheerful, alert, well-informed, pleasant, interested, friendly, and attentive.

Which people do employers tend *not* to hire? Those who are unfriendly, impatient, spaced-out, disinterested, sullen, uninformed, thoughtless, cheerless, or argumentative—*or* people who seem that way to them! Employers are *especially* unlikely to hire people they are afraid of.

Make sure that you don't present any of the negative traits we have mentioned here. Maybe you had good reasons for being angry, or depressed, or impatient the day you went for that job interview. Maybe you really have been treated unfairly, perhaps evey cruelly. Our message is simply this: Grow up! If you have emotional problems, learn not to inflict them on other people. This is especially important when you're looking for work. Don't inflict your problems on a person who is in a position to hire you.

Obvious? Sure, but there are a lot of people who haven't got the message. If you've had problems getting hired, make sure your attitude isn't getting in your way. Think positively! A cheerful and helpful approach can overcome many an obstacle.

If you have taken our advice to heart, you may now be thinking, "But how can I know if other people think I have an attitude problem? Nobody ever *said* I did, but who ever tells anyone that kind of thing? It's like telling someone that they have bad breath. No one ever does it."

Let us reassure you right away that you have already taken the first step toward resolving the problem (if there is one). You started wondering about it.

Take a good look at yourself by answering the following questions *honestly*.

1. Am I generally cheerful and optimistic in my relations with others?
2. When someone needs help, do I usually pitch in without stopping to wonder what's in it for me?
3. Am I generally satisfied with how my life is going, even though there may be some difficult spots?
4. Do I avoid saying things which give offense or hurt the feelings of others?
5. Can people count on me to do what I have agreed to do?
6. Do I notice and express gratitude when someone does something thoughtful for me?
7. Am I generally comfortable with other people, including those in positions of authority?
8. Do I have plans for some things I would like to achieve in the future?
9. Am I interested in other people, in what they are doing in their lives, even if it doesn't affect me directly?
10. When I have a job or a project, do I try to do it as well as I can, even if it is difficult?

If you were able to answer "yes" to all of these questions, your attitude is probably pretty good. If not, you have an opportunity to change your life for the better in a lot of ways. But it will take some work. (There's that word again.) If you are angry or discouraged, if you feel that life is passing you by, *get some help.*

Talk to a friend, a teacher, a pastor, a priest, a rabbi, or a professional counselor. Talk with someone you can learn to trust, someone who can help you to see yourself as you really are and to change those things which are harmful to you. Only when *you* change will your circumstances change, and that includes your employment situation.

CHAPTER 3

Assessment: "Discover your hidden talents."

It is truly amazing how many people are looking for work and think that they don't know how to do anything. How silly—and how sad! Silly, because all of them in fact know how to do many things for which other people are receiving salaries. Sad, because they don't realize this and are consequently missing out on job opportunities every day.

Just recently, we were talking with a fellow named Leroy. Leroy was—you guessed it—looking for a job.

"What kind of a job?" we asked him.

"Oh, I'll take anything I can find," Leroy replied with a shrug.

"Wrong!" we shouted (to ourselves, of course).

To Leroy, we said, "Well, okay, then tell us what you can do."

"Gee, I've never really done much to speak of. I guess that's why people keep telling me that they need somebody with more experience." Leroy carefully studied his kneecap.

"Okay," we continued, "let's try thinking about the whole thing a little differently. When you were in grade school did you ever do anything to earn money? Did you ever belong to any clubs? Did you ever help someone else to do something?"

"Well, I was just a kid then," came the reply, as though the activities of a mere child could never count for much. Leroy paused for a moment. He was thinking hard, and we just waited for what he would say next.

"As a matter of fact," he began, "I did sell some Christmas cards around the neighborhood, for a couple of years. And when I was a Boy Scout, we used to wash cars to raise money to go to the Jamboree each year."

Activity	Skills	Kinds of Work
Sold cards	record-keeping persuasion being pleasant meeting people	sales fundraising receptionist waiter complaint dept. order clerk
Washing cars	use of cleaning materials enthusiasm	car wash window-washing custodial work
Scouting	leadership planning	supervisory

Model-building	attention to
	  detail
	good with hands
		assembler in
		  factory
		mechanical
		  work

Gardening	working with
	  plants
	careful observa-
	  tion
		greenhouse
		farm work
		city park worker

Team manager	record-keeping
	scheduling
	inventory
	  control
		warehouse work
		dispatcher
		store inventory
		  work

Advertising sales	same as selling
	  cards
		same as selling
		  cards

Taking pictures	observation darkroom work use of camera	studio assistant photographer photo editor

Motor pool	same as team
	  manager
		same as team
		  manager
		auto parts clerk

making deliv- eries	driving	delivery driver

He hesitated and looked up to see whether this was the kind of thing we wanted to hear about. We smiled and nodded, and a somewhat uncertain smile crept across Leroy's face, too.

"I used to build a lot of models, mostly airplanes, you know, the kind that you control with the long wire?" We nodded again. "And in the summer, I used to help my father plant the garden. It wasn't big, but I used to take care of it all summer." Leroy was rolling right along now. "When I got to high school, I wanted to play basketball, but I was too short, so the coach let me be the manager of the team. I had to look after all the equipment and make sure that there was a bus scheduled for all the away games. And I helped to sell advertising for the yearbook in my senior year. I took a lot of pictures for it, too. I have my own little darkroom, so I saved the class quite a bit of money by developing the pictures myself."

"It sounds as though you managed to keep pretty busy after all," we said. "What did you do after you left high school?"

"Well, I couldn't find a job right away so I joined the National Guard," said Leroy. "After Basic Training they put me in the Division Motor Pool for four months ordering parts and keeping track of inventory and equipment."

"Where did you learn how to do that?" we inquired.

"Well, my dad had an old pick-up truck that used to break down all the time, and he used to let me help him work on it, so I knew the names of a lot of parts already. And as far as keeping track of equipment, that was almost the same as what I did for the basketball team."

"Did you ever learn to drive that old pick-up?" we asked.

"Yeah, I sure did," said Leroy. "In fact my dad used to let me make deliveries for Old Man Baxter who had the grocery store on the corner near our house. People would call in orders and I'd pack up the things and deliver them, and then bring the money back to Baxter. He didn't pay me much, but sometimes I got pretty good tips from his customers."

"For a person who has 'never done anything,' it seems as though you've done quite a lot," we said. "Let's see what we have here," we continued. We took out a sheet of paper and began to list all of the activities Leroy had mentioned, leaving some space after each entry. Then we went back and wrote "Activity" at the top of the sheet above the list. Opposite from the word "Activity," in the middle of the sheet, we wrote "Skills." After that we went down through the list of activities, item by item, and wrote in all the skills we could think of that were necessary to perform each activity.

Finally, we went back to the top of the page and started yet a third column with the heading "Kinds of Work," right alongside "Activity" and "Skills." For each skill (or group of skills) on the list, we wrote down the name of a kind of work for which that skill would be necessary or useful. When we had finished, we showed the list that appears on page 22 to Leroy.

While Leroy studied the list we had made, we explained that this was a pretty good way for anyone to figure out what kind of work they ought to be looking for. Leroy said that some of the things on the list weren't things that he really wanted to do. No problem, we said. You can't do everything anyway. Just pick out the two or three things you feel best about and concentrate on those. After thinking about it, Leroy decided that he would like to work in a warehouse or an auto parts store.

Now maybe you can do some of the things that Leroy could do, and maybe your skills are entirely different. No two people are exactly alike, after all. But the fact remains that everyone is able to do a lot of different things they hadn't ever even thought of before. If you're not sure what kind of work you're qualified to do—or where your interests lie—take a close look at the next page and follow the instructions carefully.

Before you make a list like the one we developed with Leroy, fill in the information listed in the chart that follows as completely as you can.

LIST OF SKILLS

Paid Work: Any full-time or part-time paying jobs you have held. Put down employment during high school, after high school, military service, etc.

a. _____

b. _____

c. _____

Unpaid Work: Jobs for which you did not receive money, at home, at school, with friends or relatives.

a. _____

b. _____

c. _____

Volunteer Work: Work you have done for organizations like the Boy Scouts, Red Cross, charities, hospitals, churches.

a. _____

b. _____

c. _____

Hobbies: Many hobbies relate directly to jobs you may not even have thought of, for example: photography, auto mechanics, stamp collecting, macramé.

a. _____

b. _____

c. _____

Clubs & Organizations: A lot of the work you may have done as a member of social service or school clubs and organizations can be counted as actual job experience.

a. _____

b. _____

c. _____

Your Other Abilities: You may not have thought of these things as work, but if you can cook, sew, garden, fix a wire, draw, entertain your baby brother or do anything else, list it here.

a. _____

b. _____

c. _____

Now you are ready to make your own list of Activities, Skills and Kinds of Work, just as we did for Leroy:

ACTIVITY (What you did)	SKILLS (How you did it)	KINDS OF WORK (Job it is like)

When you have finished this, you should have a much clearer idea of your capabilities. Your next step will be to select, as Leroy did, those things which you really *want* to do.

Now that we have outlined a simple, practical way to identify your skills, experience, and "hidden talents," we'd like to take another look at the reasons for doing it.

Q. *What's wrong with taking any job you can get?*

A. You have a right—and an obligation!—to choose what's best for you. If you were buying shoes, would you take whatever pair the salesperson handed to you? Of course not. You have your own ideas about what kind of shoe is right for you. You may not find *exactly* what you want, but if one store doesn't even come *close* to matching your taste, you'll probably go somewhere else, no matter how desperately you need the shoes.

Shopping for a new job is really not so different from shopping for new shoes, a new car, a new apartment, or a new relationship. If you don't have some idea what you want, someone *else* will make the choice for you. And they will choose not what's best for *you*, but what's best for *them*.

Q. *That's all very well, but employers really have the final say in who gets hired, don't they?*

A. No, they don't. They have the final say in who is offered a job. Only *you* can decide whether or not to accept it. If you can convince an employer that you can do what he or she needs done, there's a good chance that you'll receive an offer. But don't expect employers to decide—or figure out—what you can do. Tell them!

Q. *Are there other reasons why I should know what I'm looking for?*

A. This whole book is full of reasons, as you'll discover.

But for now, let's leave it at this: "If you don't know where you want to go, you probably won't get there."

CHAPTER 4

The Résumé
(REZ-oo-may)

We mentioned earlier that most résumés are a waste of the job-seeker's time. This does not mean that you are better off without one. On the contrary, a résumé is an essential part of *everyone's* job-seeking equipment. This includes ditch diggers, file clerks, and kitchen helpers, in addition to computer programmers and behavioral psychologists.

People who hire for entry-level or laborer positions often do not expect applicants to present a résumé. But they will certainly be impressed by the applicant who does, if the résumé is a good one.

A résumé is a very personal document. Since no two résumés are identical (nor should they be) it is impossible for us to say exactly what your résumé should look like. Only you can decide that. What we can do, however, is give you some information and general guidelines about résumés. We can also warn you about the most common mistakes people make in preparing résumés. Finally, we will show you some sample résumés, both good and not-so-good.

What should a résumé include? What should be left out?

The main purpose of a résumé is to get you an interview with someone who might hire you. In order to do this, it must present a "picture" of you as a serious candidate for a particular kind of work. It should tell only those things about you which will make the employer want to talk to you in person. A résumé does *not* tell the story of your life. It does not have to include all the jobs or training you have ever had. It doesn't even have to contain a complete list of the duties you performed at a previous job. Only those parts of your background that are somehow related to the work you are seeking now should be included.

There are two basic kinds of résumés, the chronological and the functional.

[29]

C. KENT
1600 BROADWAY
METROPOLIS, NEW YORK 10017
(212) 456-1000

OBJECTIVE   Seeking a position as free-lance crime-fighter par
                 excellence that utilizes extraordinary powers and
                 abilities

GENERAL   * Able to leap tall buidings in a single bound
                 * More powerful than a locomotive
                 * Faster than a speeding bullet
                 * Capable of unassisted terrestrial and interplanetary
                   flight
                 * Powers of x-ray vision - do not abuse in presence of
                   lovely women

RELATED EXPERIENCE

Crimefighting   * Assisted plice in hundreds of difficut cases. Always
                  brought criminal to justice with 100% efficiency for
                  over 40 years - never failed.
                * Singlehandedly eliminated all major criminals in city
                  of Metropolis.
                * Saved Metropolis from destruction on several occasions.
                * Maintained 24-hour availability for over 50 years.

Maintaining   * Worked up from cub to senior reporter in 5 years.
  Cover   * Successfully maintained disguise as mild-mannered
                  reporter which fooled everyone for over 40 years.
                * Have never missed a deadline or important story.
                * Published regularly under own by-line.

Publicity   * Have appeared in several full-length feature films.
                * Starred on radio and TV shows.
                * Appeared regularly in newspapers throughout the U.S.
                * Featured in monthly comic books for 30 years.

EMPLOYMENT HISTORY

1940-present   Senior Reporter, Daily Planet, Metropolis, NY
                Featured personality, Dell Publishing Co., New York, NY
                Self-employed Crimefighter, Metropolis, NY

EDUCATION

1939   Smallville High School, Smallville, NY
                Regents Diploma (100 average, all subjects)

                Successfully maintained discipline in all classes of
                local high school for 4 years.

REFERENCES, WRITING SAMPLES, AND DEMONSTRATION ON REQUEST

The chronological résumé describes your work experience beginning with your present or most recent position and continues with your previous job and so on back as far as you choose to go.

The functional résumé takes a different approach to your experience, which we will discuss a little later. Everyone should begin by constructing a chronological résumé.

The Chronological Résumé

This type of résumé is generally divided into several sections, each with its own name. The exact number and positioning of these sections will vary, depending on whose résumé it is, what the person has done, and what kind of work he/she is looking for.

(1) The first section (this appears at the top of all résumés) contains your name, address, and telephone number.

(2) The next section is called EMPLOYMENT OBJECTIVE or OCCUPATIONAL GOAL. It tells the reader what kind of position you are looking for. If you have a varied background and are looking for any of several different positions, you may choose to put down your specific objective in a "cover letter" rather than in the résumé itself. In this case, a short BACK-GROUND SUMMARY on the résumé will give the reader a general sense of what you can do. This will make it easier to read the part of the résumé which describes your experience and training.

For the next several sections the order is more flexible. The general rule is to list the most important things first, and by "most important things" we mean those that will help the employer to see you as a good candidate for the job you want. Some people have a lot of training for a certain kind of work. Others have less training (or none at all) but have previous experience doing the kind of work they seek. Still others may have no specific training or direct experience in a certain field, but are qualified to do the job because of skills acquired elsewhere. These are called "transferable skills." For some examples, look at the "Assessment" chapter again. Remember, the section that contains the best reasons for hiring you should come right after the EMPLOYMENT OBJECTIVE or BACKGROUND SUMMARY, if you included one, and immediately after your name and address if there is no OBJECTIVE or SUMMARY.

Please note: the sections described below are given in an order that has proven best for many people. It may or may not be best for *you*.

(3) This section may be called WORK EXPERIENCE, WORK HISTORY, or PREVIOUS EMPLOYMENT. Each job you have had is listed here with the beginning and ending dates. Start with your most recent job and work backward. Write and underline your job title. If you can think of a job title which is better than the one you had (without being misleading), use it instead. (For example: *Assistant to Chef* may be better than *Kitchen Helper*.) Below the line, write the name of the company, and the city and state where it was located. Then skip a line and write a clear description of the work you did. Begin with those activities or duties that are most closely related to the job you are looking for now. A typical entry might look like this:

6/83-9/84   ASSISTANT TO CHEF
            The Fat Cat Diner, Alton, Ill.
            Prepared salads, cooked omelets and other egg dishes, peeled and sliced vegetables, arranged servings on plates, assisted chef in kitchen.

Another version of the same entry might look like this:

6/83-9/84   The Fat Cat Diner, Alton, Ill.
            Helped out in the kitchen.

It isn't hard to see why the first of these two is more likely to get an employer's attention.

(4) The next section we would like to talk about may be called SKILLS or CAPABILITIES. This is where you can list all those things you know how to do, and are part of the job you want. It doesn't matter if you have already mentioned them somewhere else (such as in the EXPERIENCE section), but if you haven't,

then it's especially important to list them here. Here is a sample SKILLS section:

SKILLS: Home-style, short-order cooking. Set-up and serving. Preparation of most American foods, including soups, salads, grilled and roast meats, casseroles, pies and pastries, poultry, stuffings and pasta items. Work well as part of a kitchen team.

(5) If you have received specific training to do the kind of work you will be applying for, you can call the next section TRAIN-ING. If not, you can call it EDUCATION. If you didn't go beyond high school, or if your formal education is unrelated to your employment goal, you might combine the two and call this section EDUCATION and TRAINING. Mention *as specifically as possible* any formal training or courses that are related to the work you want.

Some tips for this section:

- If you didn't finish school, don't say "Completed 7th grade." Just list the school and the last year attended.
- If you are looking for a job that doesn't require a college degree, don't say you have one.
- Even if you didn't finish school and later received valuable training elsewhere, don't omit the school entirely. Just put it down last.

A typical entry:

EDUCATION AND TRAINING
            Boise Job Corps Center, Boise, Idaho
            Completed 20-month intensive course in
                Culinary Arts
            Received Diploma May 1982
                Course included instruction and practical
                experience in meal preparation, measures,
                recipe reading, and set-up.
            Peoria High School, Peoria, Ill. — 1981

(6) This section is called HOBBIES or PERSONAL INTER-ESTS and follows the preceding sections, regardless of the order you may have chosen in which to arrange them. Whatever you list here, be specific. You never know when an interviewer will share your interest in softball, salmon fishing, auto repair, or Lionel trains. Be sure to list *first* any hobby that is related to the job you want.

(7) There are several other items which may be included if they apply to you. As always, stop and consider whether they will be of interest to the employer. They include: MILITARY SER-VICE (keep it short, unless the experience or training is impor-tant), LICENSE/CERTIFICATES, COMMUNITY SERVICE, AWARDS/ACHIEVEMENTS, and finally, POSSESS OWN TOOLS (for specific trades such as mechanic, plumber, or carpenter).

There is just one more line to make your chronological résumé complete. It looks like this:

REFERENCES WILL BE FURNISHED UPON REQUEST

and should come close to the bottom of your first (and only!) page.

Do not include the names of personal or business references on your résumé. List them on a separate sheet of paper or on a 3x5 card when you go for the interview and give them to the interviewer only if you are asked to do so!

▶ WHY ONLY ONE PAGE???
MOST PEOPLE WHO RECEIVE AND READ RÉSUMÉS PREFER THEM SHORT, SPECIFIC, AND INTEREST-ING. THEY HAVE ABOUT 30 SECONDS TO SPEND ON EACH RÉSUMÉ, AND THEY WOULD RATHER NOT SPEND IT TURNING PAGES. WHATEVER YOU WANT THEM TO NOTICE SHOULD BE ON THE FIRST PAGE— AND THERE SHOULD NOT BE ANY OTHER PAGES.

Up to now we have been talking about chronological résumés. This type of résumé is best for people who have had more than one paid job, and who have no large gaps in their employment history. If most of your experience has been gained in some other way than through paid employment (as a home-maker, a volunteer, by working on cars in your back yard, through short-term temporary work, or by typing your friend's manuscript), or if there are large gaps in your work history (illness, prison, unemployment, free-lance work, self-employ-ment, etc.) you should probably consider a functional résumé, using your chronological résumé as a starting point.

The Functional Résumé

A functional résumé contains much the same information as a chronological résumé, but it is arranged differently. While the chronological résumé shows the *where and when* of your employment history, the functional résumé tries to show *what you can do,* based on all your experience. Where and when you got the experience is less important than what you can actually do.

Look again at the "ASSISTANT TO THE CHEF" entry a few pages back. Suppose this person had done all these things, not at the Fat Cat Diner, but as an inmate at the Templewood State Correctional Facility. The experience is no less real and the person *can* indeed cook, but it is foolish to advertise the fact that this skill was acquired behind bars. On a functional résumé, this entry in the EXPERIENCE section would look slightly different. Instead of the date, the type of work would be listed (without the job title). The dates, job title and location would not be given. The entry would look like this:

Cooking   Prepared salads, cooked omelets, etc.

A good functional résumé will contain several (usually three to five) such descriptions of experience or accomplishments. Each one should include important things you have done in that area, even though you may have done them at different times or in different places. Do not make a separate entry for each job, only for each function.

The part of the functional résumé we have been describing is usually called EXPERIENCE or RELATED EXPERIENCE. It takes the place of the WORK HISTORY section that appears in chronological résumés.

Some employers and other people who read résumés become suspicious when there is no mention of where the experience was gained. Unless you have really never had a "job" (as is sometimes the case with housewives), it makes sense to list PLACES WORKED, WORKSITES, or simply EMPLOYMENT as the next section on your functional résumé. It need not include all of the places you have ever worked. If you are using the functional résumé to cover up a spotty work record or a series of short-term jobs, you will not want to include dates for each place worked. Another possibility (besides not putting down anything at all) is to list the amount of time you worked at each place, for example:

(2 years)   The Red Herring, Framley, AL
(8 mos.)   Al's Hash House, Benton, CO
(1 year)   McDonald's, Farmington, ME

With the information given in this section, you should be able to put together a résumé (see the appendix for additional sample résumés) which presents a positive and convincing picture of you as a candidate for employment.

THINGS TO KEEP IN MIND

- DON'T BOX YOURSELF IN — Remember, people will inquire about the entries on your résumé. Don't put yourself in the difficult position of having to admit that they are not true.
- FIRST THINGS FIRST — Try to arrange the sections, and the entries within the sections, so that your strongest selling points appear closer to the top of the page.
- THE WHOLE PICTURE — Try to arrange the different items on your résumé so that they support each other in making you appear qualified and capable.
- THINK OF THE READER — Descriptions should be clear and specific. Don't jam things together on the page.
- ATTENTION TO DETAIL — If you are not good at spelling, grammar, punctuation, etc., get someone to check your résumé over before typing it—and afterwards, too.
- ABBREVIATIONS — In general, avoid the use of abbreviations, although such common short forms as "St." for "Street" or NY for New York (State) are okay.
- DON'T SAY TOO MUCH — Some people try to tell their whole life stories on their résumés. Don't do it! Save long, detailed accounts for the interview, where you can see if the employer is really interested.
- TELEPHONE NUMBER — If you don't have a phone, find a friend or relative who will take messages for you. Many employers won't take the time to write you a letter. No phone oftens means no interview.
- TEST AND CHANGE — Don't be afraid to change things on your résumé if it isn't working well. Any résumé can be made better once you find out how many people are reacting to it.
- IT'S YOUR RÉSUMÉ — How you feel about your résumé will have a big effect on how confident you are in your job search. Above all, be sure that your résumé says what you want it to say.

Coffee Break #1

Henry and Arlene were talking about the ideal job . . .

Henry: The ideal job for me would be some place with great pay, great hours, and super benefits.

Arlene: What about job satisfaction? Doesn't that enter into it? You know, feeling good about the job. Doing a good job and getting compliments and knowing you feel good about getting up every morning and going in to the work?

Henry: Nah. What do I care about all that. As long as the money's good and hours are short, that's all I care about. I like my free time.

Arlene: What do you mean by "free time"? To me, working doesn't mean I'm a slave on the job and once I leave the job I'm "free." It just seems to me that what you are saying is that you want the job to fit your needs rather than adapting yourself to fit the needs of the job.

Henry: Listen, Arlene. All this crap about being happy on the job is just that. Crap! Life is short. My free time is the most important thing to me.

Arlene: Wait a minute! You're right, life is too short. Especially to waste it on a job you don't like. Henry, I think you'd better stop and realize that about a third of your life is spent on some job somewhere, and you're talking about it as if it were "dead time."

Henry: Okay, you've got a point. I'll give you that. But for now, all I care about is the money. Let's face it, without money there isn't a lot you can do in this life.

Arlene: You keep talking about life and work as if they were separate issues. They're not. Work is a part of life.

[38]

What I do is who I am. Once I leave my job every day, I don't stop being who I am. People are interested in me as a person, in terms of what I do. How many times a day are you asked: "What do you do?"

Henry: More times than I care to think about. I guess you're right. So what's the ideal job?

Arlene: For me? Doing something that I feel good about. Working with people I care about. And knowing that people like and respect me as a person who does a good job. And, of course, good pay and benefits, too.

Henry: I'll buy that. How do you get the ideal job?

Arlene: Plan for it. Keep looking. And make the job you've got better. Who knows, you may already have the ideal job and not know it! Check it out!

CHAPTER 5

References and Letters of Recommendation

A letter of recommendation is a piece of paper upon which some person of note has made some positive statements about you and which may help you to get a job. The person who writes your letter may be the same person who has agreed to act as your reference, although the two don't *have* to be identical.

The difference between the meaning of "references" and the meaning of "recommendations" is worth examining:

Reference: A person to whom inquiries as to character or ability can be made.

Recommendation: An endorsement as fit, worthy, or competent for a position.

LETTERS OF RECOMMENDATION

One big difference between a reference and a letter of recommendation is this: the reference (person) can change his or her mind about you, while the letter can't. The letter also has the effect of placing the writer (yes the *writer!*) more firmly on your side. One way to lessen the bad effect of a doubtful reference (such as a former employer) is to ask for a letter of recommendation.

Note that obtaining a letter of recommendation can be one of the most positive steps toward getting a job. Not only does the person whom you have asked to write the letter become aware that you are looking for a job. He or she is also forced to think of those positive abilities and qualifications you possess. (Even if the person writes a letter that isn't an all-out endorsement, it's still okay. After all, you don't *have* to use it, and at least you now know exactly where you stand with him.)

[41]

Every person who writes a letter of recommendation for you should be considered part of your contact network and should be given a copy of your résumé. (Before writing the letter, of course!)

Letters of recommendation may be obtained from anyone—the more the better, because that means your contact network is larger. But remember, you're not going to use them all (at least not at the same time).

A final tip: if possible, have the person write the letter on letterhead stationery—it's more impressive that way.

THE IMPORTANCE OF REFERENCES

Questions and Answers
Q. *What is a reference?*
A. A reference is the name, address, phone number, and often also the position or profession of a person who is willing (and able) to give specific and positive information about you to a prospective employer.

Q. *What kind of information is this person supposed to give about me?*
A. Different employers want to know different things. Basically, they want to be reassured that you will be a good employee if they hire you. For example, they want to know whether you will show up for work regularly and on time. They want to be sure that you won't steal from them, that you will get along with the other people working there (including supervisors), and that you aren't afraid to work. They will probably also ask questions about information that you have put down on an application form.

Q. *What kind of person should I ask to give information about me?*
A. It should be someone, first of all, who is actually available for comment. A person who would say all sorts of good things about you, but who is never there to answer the phone, is not a good reference. Also, people who live or work too far away are not good because your potential employer may not be willing to make long distance tele-

phone calls. Some examples of good references are business and community leaders, former supervisors or co-workers, priests or pastors, former teachers, fellow volunteers, and other established community residents who know you and think well of you. Social workers, counselors, parole officers, and other professionals who have worked with you *may* be okay for some positions. But before you list them, consider the employer's reaction when he or she calls your reference on the phone and is greeted with "Department of Social Services" or "Probation and Parole." Use common sense!

Q. *How many names do I need on my list of references?*
A. The more the better. That way you can choose the best ones to put down for each job you apply for. If you know someone who works for the company to which you are applying, list that person. On the other hand, if your best reference is on vacation, don't use him/her.

Q. *Is it okay to list my references right on my résumé?*
A. No. You don't want the employer to check your references before you even get to the interview. That simply wouldn't be fair to you.

Q. *So all I really have to do is make a list of the names of people I think would give me a good recommendation, right?*
A. Wrong! You have to *talk* with each of the people before you put them down on your list and get their permission to do so. Better yet, give the people an idea about what kind of work you are seeking and show them a copy of your résumé.

Q. *This all sounds pretty complicated. Are references really a must?*
A. That depends. Do you really want to get a job?

See the Appendix for examples.

CHAPTER 6

Resources

In any community, there are many places where you can go to find job leads. Most of the organizations involved are there to help people. Generally, they provide their services free of charge. These services often include job leads, career counseling, aptitude testing, vocational skills training, and educational programs.

Job-seekers should be aware, however, that although community-based organizations (CBOs) offer free services, the quality of their services is sometimes less than useful. The information they pass along is often incorrect, inadequate, outdated, or completely misleading.

Bear in mind that what you are primarily looking for are *job leads*, and not necessarily more advice. When making the rounds of CBOs, the job-seeker's perception is often that these organizations are more concerned with adding to their client population than providing information which may be immediately put to use.

Please do not take this to mean CBOs are worthless. They are useful when you understand their mission in relation to your objective. You want to get a job; you want them to help you. Don't depend completely on others when it comes to getting a job. Enlist their help and support but trust *only* your own instincts. You are an expert on yourself!

Consider this: all rip-offs aren't committed in terms of money. If someone (or some institution) gives you bad advice and sends you on wild-goose chases, they are stealing your time. That is time you might have spent earning money!

Another potential resource is an employment consultant or private employment agency. If what they are offering is free, take it. Be very careful when they start talking about money. Some companies have charged job-seekers thousands of dollars for counseling, coaching, testing, résumé preparation, and a multitude of services which have resulted in no jobs and empty pockets. Most of the time and money was spent in preparing the person to *look* for a job. When complaints were pursued in court, the agencies stated that they had made *no* guarantees.

Think about it. With very few exceptions, who can guarantee that you will *get* a job? (The one notable exception is YOU.)

When dealing with any private agency, don't sign anything or pay any money unless they can absolutely guarantee you (through a written contract) that they can place you in a job.

If they can't guarantee to place you in a job, ask them what exactly they are offering.

The foregoing may seem like a very long warning label, but its major purpose is to make you aware that you are in charge. You can pick and choose. You do not have to take anyone's advice (not even ours). If someone wants to take control of your job search, ask yourself, "Why?" What's in it for them? What's in it for you? Remember, you are the most important person in this situation.

As you examine the following resources list, test each one with: "What's in it for me?"

JOB LEADS, CAREER COUNSELING, REFERRALS, ETC.
(Note: The page colors mentioned in the "Where to Find Them" sections refer to page colors in your local telephone directory.

RESOURCES WHICH ARE FREE OF CHARGE
State Employment Agencies
Even though only a small percentage of job-seekers find jobs through the State Job Service, be sure to register here and try your best to *get to know one of the interviewers*. The best way to get a job through these agencies is to check the job listings regularly (if available) and to stay in close touch with the interviewer. State Job Service listings can sometimes also be found in such places as public libraries, adult education centers, veterans' centers, and the like. If you manage to establish a rapport with your contact at the State Job Service, you might even be able to register for job interviews by phone. Since the number of people referred to a particular job is small, the competition is not so fierce once you

get the interview. If you succeed in becoming a favorite of your Job Service contact, you might even find out about jobs that are not on the official listing yet; the ones that have just come in that day, too soon to be included, or jobs the interviewer has heard about through the office grapevine. Qualified, low-income applicants may be able to obtain a TJTC (Targeted Jobs Tax Credit) Voucher from their nearest Job Service office. This paper may help you to land a job because it provides a tax advantage to the person or company who hires you. Show it to potential employers during the interview. Remember, the TJTC credit is only good if you have signed up *before* your first day of work.
Where to find them: In the Blue Pages under State Department of Labor.

Job Information Centers

Many public libraries (especially the main branches in larger urban areas) have job information or career development centers. You can save money by using their newspapers and checking their Job Service listings. Some employers will post jobs on bulletin boards in these areas. Civil service job openings are often listed here, too. You may find also books and pamphlets with job and career information at these centers. Some even offer résumé assistance and career counseling, either in groups or on an individual basis.
Where to find them: In the White Pages under your local public library.

Human Services Agencies

In many urban and heavily populated areas there are community centers, Urban League offices, counseling centers, drug rehabilitation programs, centers for women, etc. Some of these places have counselors who really know what they are doing.
Where to find them: Go to a local library and ask for a Human Services Directory or any listing of Human Services agencies.

Veterans' Centers

There are Vet Centers all over the country. The Vietnam Era veteran, for example, can find a wide range of services which include job listings, personal counseling, crisis counseling, educational and career advice.

Where to find them: In the White Pages under Vet Center.

Classified Ads

This is the hardest way to find a job. *Everybody* uses the help-wanted ads! Sunday issues of local newspapers are usually the best because they contain the largest number of listings. If the ad includes a phone number, you had better start dialing early on the first day the ad appears. A touch-tone phone will be handy to have because you may have to do a lot of dialing before you get through. It doesn't hurt to submit your résumé to those places requesting it, but only respond to the ads that list a specific company name. So-called "blind" ads which list only P.O. Box number are usually a waste of time at best.

Only about 5% of all jobs are found through the classified advertising section. Sometimes small local weekly newspapers are a better source of leads because there is less competition.

Civil Service Offices

The governments of villages, towns, cities, counties, and individual states (and also the federal government) are usually required to make their job openings known to the public. You'll find these openings posted on the main bulletin board in almost all government buildings and usually at Job Information Centers in the local library. To get your own copies of job offerings, examination announcements, sample test questions, and application forms, you can also go directly to the local civil service office. As a rule, this can be found in the town or city hall, the county courthouse, county, state or federal office buildings, or in post offices.

If you are in a hurry to get a job, you will encounter a lot of frustration using this approach. It can take up to six months before you even hear anything about the job you applied for. However, if you are a person who performs well on tests, take every one for which you qualify. Maybe one of those jobs will come through six months or even a year later when you really need it. Many civil service tests are given on the weekend, so you can try for a government position while still holding down your current job. As far as salaries are concerned, the rule of thumb is: the larger the government, the larger the salary. But bear in mind that the competition for these jobs is usually stiff.

Where to find them: In the Blue Pages under the name of your village or town. For a city, county, state, or U.S. Government job, look under Civil Service Commission (or Dept.) which is listed alphabetically after the name of the government branch.

College Placement Offices

Almost all colleges have placement libraries with information about specific companies and other organizations that recruit on campus. Even if you never attended the school in question, it might be worth your while to investigate these career development centers. There may be a bulletin board which, in addition to specific job listings, will have the dates on which interviews are scheduled with company recruiters or personnel officers. You can write to these people, send your résumé, and tell them that you, too, would like an interview while they are in the area.

If you did attend the school, you are eligible for a variety of services which will include counseling, interview scheduling, and the mailing of transcripts and recommendations. You can use these services for many years after you graduate.

Bulletin Boards

Bulletin boards are everywhere: in community centers, laundromats, supermarkets, restaurants, schools, college student centers and faculty office buildings, post offices, churches, factories—the list is almost endless. You will find all sorts of things posted there, job openings not the least among them.

Job Clubs

A job club is a group approach to finding work. Members of the group make a commitment to meet regularly and provide support, information, and assistance to one another in their job search. Help with résumés, letters, interviewing, and above all, encouragement is what you will find here. The approach is successful when the members work hard and cultivate positive attitudes. When the group begins to swap tales of woe, productivity is quickly lost. Make sure the group you join is really serious about finding work, and not just lamenting their fate.

Where to find them: Job clubs are operated by a number of agencies throughout the U.S. Ask at your library's Job Information Center, the county or city manpower program, or the State Job Service. If you cannot find a job club in your area, you can start your own by writing to the authors of this book for further information.

The Welfare Department

Most welfare departments have an employment unit or offer some form of job search assistance. Other kinds of assistance may include free day care and counseling. Welfare departments are uncomfortable to deal with because of the kind of information they are required to obtain about their clients, but if you really hit rock bottom, they can help you get moving again.

Where to find them: In the Blue Pages under County Social Services.

Armed Forces

Military service isn't the right choice for everyone, but it can keep you going and provide you with some training to get you started when you are discharged. Prior to enlistment, make it a point to find out the most promising areas for future employment in the civilian sector, and get training that applies to them while you are in the service. Be sure to get a *written guarantee* of the kind of training you will receive. Verbal promises or agreements don't count! The pay isn't bad for new recruits and, of course, most of your daily needs such as food and housing are taken care of.

Where to find them: In the Blue Pages under U.S. Government Offices. Look for the branch of service that interests you (Army, Navy, Air Force, Marine Corps, Coast Guard).

RESOURCES WHICH ARE NOT FREE OF CHARGE
Private Employment Agencies

Private agencies work for employers. They try to find specific kinds of employees for them. If you do not happen to possess the background they are looking for, there won't be much they can do for you. Even if you *do* have the right background there is a chance that the agency will charge *you* (not the employer) a hefty fee for its "service." If the employer is desperate for help, he/she may agree to pay the agency fee if you are hired. We recommend that you insist on accepting only such "fee-paid" positions. Be careful when you sign and remember: very few people find jobs this way!

Where to find them: In the Yellow Pages under "Employment Agencies."

Private Career Counseling

Here you pay to explore your career goals, that is, to find out what you want to do and what kind of work would make you happy. These companies cannot promise job placements and may have to state that in their advertising. We advise extreme caution! Some of these companies charge thousands of dollars! You may pay a lot of money and leave just as confused as you were when you came in.

Where to find them: In the Yellow Pages under "Vocational Guidance."

CAREER COUNSELING, APTITUDE TESTING, JOB TRAINING, JOB INFORMATION, EDUCATION

SOURCES WHICH ARE FREE OF CHARGE
Adult Education Centers

These centers are to be found in many larger cities. Most are very well run and offer their clients a wide range of educational services. They usually also offer aptitude testing, vocational and academic counseling, federal manpower program information, civil service test preparation, and much more. Class size tends to be small so teachers really have time to teach. Many Adult Education Centers offer both daytime and evening classes.

Where to find them: Contact your local Board of Education or school district administration as listed in the White Pages or the State Education Department in the Blue Pages.

On-The-Job Training

This opportunity is offered by all counties and many larger cities as a part of their federal manpower program. While you are working at a regular job, federal funds are used to reimburse the employer for half of your salary for a period of six months. If you are eligible for this program you can provide the employer with a strong incentive to hire you and save a lot of money. It is especially worth looking into if you have learned a trade in school but have no on-the-job experience. Be aware that you *must* be declared eligible before starting work.

Where to find it: In the Blue Pages under "Employment and Training" in the city or county listings.

Job Corps

This is a federally funded program for persons aged 16 to 21. It offers vocational training and GED preparation at various centers around the country. You can either live there or commute from home. This is an excellent way to get started if you are a high school dropout.

Where to find it: In the White Pages under Job Corps Centers.

Union Apprenticeship Programs

These are excellent programs but the number of openings is very limited, especially in trades which are currently not in great demand (rough carpentry, for example). Classroom training is provided along with on-the-job instruction, and trainees are paid for their time. Primarily, these programs are intended for individuals between 17 and 26 years of age.

Where to find them: In the Blue Pages under State Department of Labor.

High School Guidance Offices

If you are currently in school, or are a recent graduate, you should keep in touch with these people. They may be a good source of career and job information.

How to find them: In the White Pages under Board of Education or School District.

SOURCES WHICH ARE NOT FREE OF CHARGE
Community and Junior Colleges

If you choose your field carefully, you can often get a better-paying job nowadays with a two-year associate's degree than with a four-year bachelor's degree. Check with the college placement office to find out which fields of study are leading to well-paying jobs after graduation. Currently, technical fields such as electronics and computers appear to be promising. Colleges often maintain very productive relationships with local businesses and can be helpful in placing their graduates. Before you start, though, find out not only what training you will get, but what you can expect when you finish.

Where to find them: In the Yellow Pages under "Schools" or in the White Pages under the name of the college.

Trade, Technical, and Business Schools

There are over 7,000 of these schools with more than 600 work-related majors. But be careful—some of them offer training for jobs which don't exist. Some of them, on the other hand, are truly excellent. Check with your local high school guidance office, Adult Education Center, or State Education Dept. to find out which schools are really useful.

Where to find them: In the Yellow Pages under "Schools."

We are aware that not all of the information presented here will be of immediate use to you. We hope, though, that you will review it in the future to remind yourself of all the opportunities available in the area of career development. We also hope that you have read this section with a *positive* attitude, looking for ideas that can help you with your job search and simply ignoring those that don't apply to you. Remember, a positive attitude is the first and foremost requirement for the serious job-seeker.

BEFORE   DURING   AFTER

CHAPTER 7
Research

**WHAT YOU NEED TO KNOW BEFORE YOU APPLY—
AND HOW TO FIND OUT**

By now you should have a pretty clear idea of the kind of work you will be looking for. You should also have some ideas about how to find the names of some companies, businesses, or organizations that hire people with your skills. But before you make a list of these companies and start rushing around town knocking on doors, stop and think. Do you know everything you need to know about these companies in order to be really convincing when you get there? What *do* you need to know?

Angelo has just gotten out of the service where he drove heavy trucks for two years. He remembers seeing a big plant on the north side of town and decides to see whether they can use a driver. He drives out and, sure enough, there's a big sign that says "Well-Bilt Manufacturing, Inc." But Angelo soon discovers that there's nobody there. He goes to a gas station next door to the plant and the attendant tells him that "Well-Bilt" has moved to the next town down the river. So he drives down and, after asking around town, finds the new plant. He sees a big sliding door with a truck backed up to it and goes over. "Can I talk to the boss of the shipping department?" he asks one of the workers. "He ain't here this afternoon," is the answer. "He should be in tomorrow around ten."

The next day at ten o'clock, Angelo is back at Well-Bilt, talking with the shipping supervisor. "I just got out of the service and I'm looking for a job as truck driver," says Angelo. "I'd like to help you out, pal—I was a driver in the service myself, but we don't run any trucks here," says the supervisor. "We just get the orders ready for pick-up." "Oh," says Angelo. "Well, thanks anyway." Angelo leaves, disappointed. He never finds out that the company is looking for two forklift operators. The supervisor never finds out that Angelo was one of the best forklift operators in his supply company in the service.

What Should Angelo Have Done?

Angelo should have been more aware of all the different things he can do and then gone to the *right place* and talked with the *right person*. Think back to Chapter 4 where we talked about discovering your hidden talents. If Angelo had been on his toes, he might well have been hired as a forklift operator.

If you have gone through the steps in Chapter 4, it is now time to start collecting information about the places you want to work. This requires careful planning. The 3x5 card system is the easiest way to organize your research.

```
                      (FRONT)
Carroll Mfg. Co., Auburn, NY
342-5555                           J. Carroll, Pres.
Contact: Bill Prie, Purchasing
Mfr. of sm. parts for outboard motors &
fittings for skis.
56 employees, avg.                      $14,000/a
```

```
                      (BACK)
7/ 9/86   ....Ltr. of Inquiry to ad
7/12/86   ....Phone call to Mr. Prie, told me
              to call again
7/13/86   ....Sent résumé
7/16/86   ....Phoned Prie, appt. scheduled
              for 7/18/86
7/18/86   ....Good interview, will call me
              by 7/25
7/19/86   ....Thank-you note sent
```

Select a number of companies or organizations that you would like to work for. Before you approach them, go to the library and begin your research. When you are doing your "homework," remember, everything you can find out is important. It makes no difference whether the information was found in the newspaper, in a company newsletter, or overheard at a party. Be alert and make notes on everything.

◗ TO REALLY EXPLORE THE HIDDEN JOB MARKET, APPLY TO COMPANIES BECAUSE YOU *WANT TO WORK FOR THEM*, AND *NOT* BECAUSE THEY HAPPEN TO HAVE AN AD IN THE PAPER. BEAT THE COMPETITION!

Three-by-five cards are very portable. Don't leave home without them! They will provide an ongoing record of your job-search activities. Along the way some will be discarded, while new ones will constantly be added.

SOURCES

We have compiled a list of 20 sources of information to get you started in developing your own job leads. These directories and other materials are available at your library or newsstand.

Because of space limitations we cannot tell you everything about each directory we mention, but we will try to give you the highlights as they pertain to the Hidden Job Market. All of them contain such basic information as the names of companies and brief descriptions of company products or services.

Polk City Directory

Contains names and titles of many important businesspeople as well as the products or services which their companies offer. Good for finding directions to places of business, because it lists names of surrounding businesses, street descriptions, and intersections. Also lists all area phone numbers in numerical sequence, so that you may be able to find the locations of "blind," box-number ads.

McRae's State Industrial Directories

Companies are listed by name, region, and product. Other information includes annual gross sales; date company was started; plant and property size; number of employees; names and titles of company officers; locations of branches.

McRae's Blue Book

Same as previous entry, but at a national, rather than a state, level. Volume 5 has large, complete display ads placed by industrial companies. Gives an excellent idea of current company philosophy and product line.

1986 Thomas Register

Details products and services of American manufacturers. Other registers in this series include "Company Profiles" and "Catalogues of Companies." Very good source of information on current thinking and direction of companies, also lists products or services. *Thomas Registers* do not contain names of company personnel.

Moody's Industrial Manual

Contains a well-rounded, detailed company description, if you don't mind wading through a lot of complicated financial information. Categories include "The Business and What it Does"; history; properties; subsidiaries; list of management personnel.

Standard and Poor's Register

Volume I tells about corporations and gives the names, titles, and functions of 400,000 officers, directors, and other key personnel. It describes products and services, gives annual sales figures and the number of employees, and also lists division names and functions, principal business affiliations, and the addresses of executives.

Volume II gives detailed information on 70,000 corporation directors and executives. Listings include: title, business and home address; year and place of birth; college attended and year of graduation; memberships in fraternal organizations. This one is truly a goldmine!

Volume III lists corporations by general group (i.e., type of business), location, and corporate structure (i.e., subsidiaries, divisions, affiliations).

◗ THE LIBRARY IS ONE OF YOUR BEST FRIENDS WHEN YOU ARE LOOKING FOR WORK.

Manning Business Telephone Directory

Detailed listings for local businesses that offer products and services to other companies. Listings are arranged by company name and by type of product or service. This directory is available for most major population areas.

All-in-One Directory

This source book of media and press information lists business, trade, and black newspapers by category. TV stations as well as AM and FM radio stations are listed geographically.

National Directory of Addresses and Telephone Numbers

Contains every important address and phone number you might want. The ten subsections are: Business and Finance; Professional Business Services; Government; Politics and Diplomacy; Education; Foundations; Religious Denominations; Hospitals; Hot Lines and Social Services; Associations and Unions; Transportation and Hotels; Communications and Media; Culture and Recreation; Business Services. Alphabetical listings are also included. A fascinating look at American institutions.

Million Dollar Directory

Lists 120,000 businesses with a net worth of more than $500,000 including manufacturing companies, utilities, transportation, banks and trust companies, mutual funds, brokerage firms, insurance companies, wholesalers, and retailers. Also gives the names of company officers. Company listings are alphabetical by location and product/service classification.

Kelly's Manufacturers' and Merchants' Directory

This reference work is divided into three sections. The first lists manufacturing, merchandising, and wholesaling firms which offer industrial services. The second has a classified ads trade section, and the third contains a list of exporters and services.

Standard Directory of Advertisers

Lists the names of top company executives as well as other company officials from Marketing and Advertising Director to head of Manufacturing Operations for major companies nationwide. A terrific source of names.

▶ REMEMBER!
WHEREVER YOU FIND SOME OF THE DIRECTORIES
WE HAVE LISTED, YOU WILL ALSO FIND MUCH
MORE INFORMATION IN THE FORM OF REGIONAL,
COUNTY, AND LOCAL DIRECTORIES, REPORTS, SUR-
VEYS, AND OTHER DOCUMENTS.

Annual Reports *(published by specific corporations)*
Contain much useful information about company performance, philosophy, goals, and new product lines. Reading such reports is an absolute must for anyone interested in getting a job with a specific corporation.

Congressional Yellow Book
Gives details of Congressional agencies and departments. Lists individual names, phone numbers, and brief job descriptions for all congressional staff.

Federal Yellow Book
Same as above for all federal departments and agencies.

State Government Phone Directories *(for each state)*
Every state issues its own directory which lists all employees by name, department, and phone number, as well as an organizational section which lists key staff by department.

Taylor's Encyclopedia of Government Officials
(federal and state)
Lists all elected officials (both federal and state) by branch of government and department or agency.

Encyclopedia of Associations
A comprehensive source of detailed information about American non-profit organizations of national scope. Tells location, size, objectives, and much more for 15,000 trade associations, professional societies, labor unions, fraternal and patriotic organizations, chambers of commerce, etc.

CHAPTER 8
Networking

Networking is the skill of expanding personal contacts to get what you want. Businessmen network. Politicians network. Policemen and religious leaders network. Everybody networks to a greater or lesser degree, and you can network, too.

If you have three friends, and each of these people has three friends, and you contact each of them, the odds are pretty good that each of the nine you are now dealing with will also have three friends. This progression goes on and on.

Networking is the art of stringing contacts together so that eventually you can reach anybody.

You say you don't know people in high places (or the places you want to get to)? People in high places always know someone who is socially or economically less well off than they are. And as individuals, we always know someone who is better off than we are. The trick is to connect the middle contacts. Through the networking process you can reach anybody: a boss, a baker, the President of the United States, the Pope.

Getting a job is a process of social interaction. Human beings are connected to one another by invisible, unmeasured pathways. Everybody counts, because everybody knows someone. Everybody.

▶ ASK EVERYBODY!
NEVER SELL ANYONE SHORT. YOU NEVER KNOW WHOM THEY MIGHT KNOW. KEEP ASKING EVERYONE WHAT KIND OF WORK THEY DO AND WHERE THEY DO IT. TELL THEM WHAT YOU DO. ASK THEM WHOM THEY KNOW. LISTEN!
   ACT!!!

◗ KEEPING IT A SECRET
THE NUMBER-ONE FAILURE OF PEOPLE LOOKING
FOR WORK IS NOT TELLING OTHER PEOPLE THAT
THEY ARE LOOKING. THAT MEANS *INDIVIDUALS*,
NOT AGENCIES.

You can develop your own personal contact network. By using the following "Who Do You Know" list, you can expand your circle of acquaintances. Some of them may know about job openings. Others may actually be in a position to interview and hire you. You may not know somebody in every category of the list, but surely you will know at least some people in some of the categories. And you can get to know others. Remember, almost half of all people working said that they found their jobs by knowing someone, someone who was in the right place at the right time to be helpful to them.

Before you continue, it's time for an "Attitude Check." Have any of the following questions or doubts occurred to you as you were reading this chapter?

1. I've already tried this and it doesn't work.
2. I don't like to depend on other people for help.
3. People don't want to be bothered with my problems.
4. What if I just don't know many people?
5. It's hard to admit that I'm not working, especially to people I don't know really well.

If you are thinking this way, you are probably setting yourself up for failure. Don't do it!

There is plenty of productive work for you to do, and setting up roadblocks for yourself won't help you to get it done.

Here is our response to each of the "roadblocks" above:

1. We've heard this one from a lot of people. Some were just plain wrong in their approach ("You don't happen to know about any jobs, do you?"), others gave up the first (or tenth) time they heard the word "No." Networking works, but you have to do it *right* and you have to do *enough* of it.
2. And what will you be doing if you don't get a job?
3. If approached properly, most people are more than willing to be helpful if they can. Wouldn't you be?
4. Then get to know more people.
5. First, it's only hard if you decide to let it be hard. Others will seldom judge you as harshly as you judge yourself. (Except, perhaps, relations who are supporting you!). You are working at finding the right job. (You wouldn't be reading this if you weren't.)

So, how's your attitude doing?

THE "WHO DO YOU KNOW" LIST

Make a complete list of all the people you know in each of the following categories. Add any other categories you can think of. Put down *everyone*, including the ones who are not working—they may still be able to provide you with valuable information.

These are the people you know personally (although you need not know them all that well), or the people you have at least met at some time in the past. People you know or have met are valuable to you in your job search, because they will be more inclined to help you than will total strangers. (Remember, though, that many of the people you are friendly with now were total strangers when you first became acquainted with them. It isn't a permanent condition.) Ask them to talk with their co-workers, employers, friends, relatives—with their own contacts —to see whether these people know about any job openings for which they could recommend you.

FAMILY: mother, father, husband/wife, brothers, sisters.

RELATIVES: grandparents, aunts, uncles, nephews, nieces, cousins, in-laws.

FRIENDS: girlfriends, boyfriends, best friends, acquaintances.

NEIGHBORS: people you live near, former neighbors who have moved but still live locally.

ROOMMATES: past or present, often willing to be helpful.

FORMER CO-WORKERS: either from paid or from volunteer positions, regardless of whether they are still working in the same place as where you got to know them. They can recommend you to new bosses as well as to old ones.

FORMER CLASSMATES AND TEACHERS: from whatever schools you attended. Also members of school organizations, clubs or extra-curricular activities groups, the Alumni Association, the Reunion Committee.

High School: look through your old yearbook; it will help you to remember their names.

Trade School or College: likely to be employed, good contacts.

Instructors: a good source of information because they may know other professional people. Always ready to help if they can. (Did you think they were in it for the money?)

CLERGY: your rabbi, pastor, or priest knows a lot of people and would be pleased to arrange introductions for you.

PARTYGOERS: remember the names and get the numbers of people you have met socially. This great opportunity often passes unused.

FELLOW TEAM MEMBERS OR SPORTSMEN: if you play on any teams or go hunting or fishing with others, you're probably on special terms with them. Let them know about your situation.

CHURCH: besides the clergy, how about the other members of the congregation? Ever sing in the choir? Belong to a youth or couples group? How about the Building Committee? If you've never gotten involved . . . why not start now?

CLUBS, ASSOCIATIONS, VOLUNTEER GROUPS: space does not allow us to include a complete list of all civic, religious, fraternal, social or charitable organizations. Here are just a few examples of the more common ones. Spread the word among the memberships:

> Lions; Kiwanis; Rotary; League of Women Voters; Unions; Neighborhood Associations; Knights of Columbus; Veterans' Organizations; Volunteer Fire Department; Ladies Auxiliary; PTA; Literacy Volunteers; Scouts; Museums; Health Clubs; Fundraising Committees; Political Parties; Special Interest Organizations (Hiking, Hobbies, Conservation, Bridge, Poker, Singing Groups, Auto Clubs, Motorcycle Clubs); you can see how the list could really be almost endless.

COMMUNITY BUSINESS PEOPLE: These people are interested in your good will because they are interested in your continuing patronage. Their contacts are most likely to be among the most useful to you. Here are just a few examples of possible contacts:

> your lawyer, filling station attendant, store manager, doctor, banker, dentist, baker, landlord, insurance agent, letter carrier, waiter/waitress, mechanic, cab driver, delivery person, shopkeeper, grocer, repairperson, plumber, income tax preparer, accountant, dry cleaner, electrician, real estate broker, bus driver, salesperson, printer, tree surgeon, exterminator, restaurant proprietor.

And here, step by step, is what to do:

List the name, address, and phone number of each person you can think of, and keep adding to the list as new names occur to you or you meet new people. Don't exclude anyone—you never know whom a person might know.

Contact each person on your list and . . .

Tell each one what you are looking for.

Give each a copy of your résumé.

Ask each for advice and assistance.

Get letters of recommendation from them.

Be friendly and be a good listener. People will help you if you make the effort to show your appreciation, not just for their good advice and truly helpful tips, but for their time. Don't be afraid to say "thank you" even if their assistance doesn't turn out to be very helpful today. Tomorrow it might get you a job!

Stay in close touch with your contacts until you've found a job and let them know that you are still looking.

◗ CROSS-COUNTRY NETWORKING

EVER HEARD THE STORY ABOUT THE CROSS-COUNTRY TELEPHONE WAGER THAT WAS BEGUN ONE EVENING IN NEW YORK CITY? THE IDEA WAS TO SEE WHICH OF TWO TEAMS WOULD BE FIRST TO PLACE AN UNINTERRUPTED SERIES OF LOCAL TELEPHONE CALLS FROM COAST TO COAST. HERE'S THE WAY IT WORKED: THE FIRST CALL WAS TO A FRIEND IN THE NEXT ADJACENT AREA CODE. THIS PERSON WAS ASKED TO CALL SOMEONE HE KNEW IN THE NEXT ADJACENT AREA CODE, AND SO FORTH ACROSS THE COUNTRY. THE WINNER WAS PROCLAIMED BY SOMEONE FROM CALIFORNIA CALLING COLLECT TO THE ORIGINATING NUMBER AND ASKING FOR MR. ALPHA. (THE SECOND TEAM WAS MRS. BETA.) IT TOOK ONLY THREE HOURS AND 17 MINUTES FOR AN AMUSED GENTLEMAN FROM FRESNO, CAL. TO CALL AND ASK FOR MR. ALPHA.

NOW, THAT'S NETWORKING!

CHAPTER 9

Going Directly to the Employer

One of the easiest ways to get a job, believe it or not, is by going directly to the employer and asking for a job. In the 1979 U.S. Dept. of Labor study, 24% of the people who had gotten jobs stated that they had succeeded in this manner.

◗ THE AVERAGE JOB TURN-OVER IS ONCE EVERY THREE YEARS. GO TO YOUR LOCAL LIBRARY. CHECK THE MICRO-FILMS FOR HELP-WANTED ADS IN THE SUNDAY PAPERS THREE YEARS AGO. APPLY FOR THE JOBS YOU FIND LISTED THERE. *THEY MIGHT BE OPEN AGAIN!*

What is meant by "going directly to the employer"?

It means not waiting for an ad to appear or for a job to be listed with the state job service or even to be referred by an employment agency, friend or anyone else.

It simply means approaching an employer and saying:

"Hello, my name is Bob. I'm a writer, I've done short stories, poems, technical reports and news releases. I've had experience in all of the media and I'd like to talk with you. Could I make an appointment with you at your earliest convenience?"

An employer can be approached over the phone (which is one of the most effective ways), through a letter, or in person.

Personnel specialists (and other traditionalists) often object to these methods. The question is: Why do they object?

Let's look at the so-called "normal" approach to getting a job. You go to the personnel office and they hand you an application. If it isn't for a position they are actively seeking to fill, it is put into the "pending" file. Usually, you will be considered for only the job you wrote down where the application says:

Position Desired: _____

If you leave this blank, you may as well never have applied. If you put down several positions, you will be classified as:

"unspecified."

There are many different things that might happen to your application, but you should be getting the general picture by now. If the personnel people are doing their jobs, namely screening applications, the chances are very good that you will never get to see the person who has the power to hire you.

What to do? Well, simply go around, or under, or over the personnel office. It doesn't matter, as long as you get the interview.

The telephone is one of the best ways of approaching an employer directly. But never tell anyone that you are looking for "a job," "a position," "employment," or "work." If you are speaking with a secretary or a receptionist and the idea is to get an interview with the boss, you must be willing to take a gamble.

You might say: "I'm returning a call from Mr. Brown."

Or you could try. "Hi, is Jim in?" referring to Mr. Brown by his first name.

How about: "This is in reference to an idea that could be worth thousands of dollars to Mr. Brown." (If he hires you and you produce, he could make thousands of dollars.)

Let's suppose you call and are told that Mr. Brown is not in, but you feel that this is not the truth. Have someone else call and say that they have a special delivery package and then ask:

"When will he be in?"

◆ IF YOU DON'T GET THE JOB, YOUR FACE WILL BE RED FOR A SHORT WHILE. IF, ON THE OTHER HAND, YOU DO GET THE JOB, YOUR FACE WILL BE PINK. WITH PLEASURE!

If you find that he is indeed in, or will be in at a certain time, try calling back and dialing the next digit. For example, if you dialed 555-1231 the first time you called, this time try the number 555-1232. Quite often, this will ring directly into the boss's office (or the office of some other executive who will then transfer your call).

Here is another approach along the same lines. If you learn that the boss is going to be in at a certain time, you can deliver your application or résumé in person (in a large manila envelope marked "Personal—Hand Carry only").

Sometimes you will be asked over the phone to send in your résumé. You can take this to mean "drop off" your résumé and try to get an interview at that time.

There are two things you should know about personnel workers:

• They are generally the last people to know about job openings. Line workers, supervisors, foremen know first.

• The personnel office does not make the actual decision to hire. They may make recommendations, but the boss is the one who really makes the decision.

If you want to beat the odds in the employment game, you can't let employers have everything their way. *All the rules favor employers.* After all, who do you think made up the rules in the first place? *Moral of the story: learn to break the rules and win the game.*

According to the rules you file an application, send in a résumé, make polite inquiries, and are constantly told that you will be called in for an interview. All you have to do is sit by the phone and wait patiently for that call.

HORSEFEATHERS!

Go in for an interview. Tell them you were called. Tell them a message was left for you. In any event, here you are. Hang in there until they interview you or give you a definite day and time for an interview. If you feel you are worth it, take the chance.

BE ASSERTIVE!

> ◗ OUR DICTIONARY DEFINES ASSERTIVE PEOPLE AS THOSE WHO " . . . MAKE BOLD OR CONFIDENT STATEMENTS ABOUT THEIR CAPABILITIES."

The following telephone script was created with the idea of letting your voice "do the walking." First, list all the places you want to call. Then rehearse the script by reading it aloud several times. When you feel comfortable with it, try it. What does it matter if you strike out the first few times? Keep trying. You will improve with time. Get a friend or relative to help you. *Be confident! Be persistent!*

THE TELEPHONE SCRIPT

Introduce yourself!
Hello! My name is _____. *May I have the name of the person in charge of the* _____ *department?*
When you get this name, write it down. _____
Now use it!
Thank you, may I speak to _____?

Introduce yourself!
Hello, Mr./Ms. _____, *my name is* _____. *I am a* _____.
At this point you have about a minute to state your qualifications. Write them down beforehand. Be brief! Remember: you are selling yourself!

_____

_____

_____

_____

Ask for an interview!
The interview! This is the whole point of the call.
May I have an interview with you at your earliest convenience?

If you are refused an interview, try this approach:
Could I come in and speak to you anyway . . . in case anything comes up?

If you are refused again, try this option:
Could I see you for just a few minutes . . . so that you'll be aware of me . . . in the event of any future opportunities?

Ask for a referral!
Could you suggest any other places I could contact?
ASK . . . ASK . . . ASK.
Could you give me the name and the phone number of the person I should contact?
ASK . . . ASK . . . ASK.
May I use your name when I call?
ASK . . . ASK . . . ASK.
May I check back with you? (If so, when?)
ASK . . . ASK . . . ASK.

If all of these approaches fail, go to this:
May I send you my résumé?

Coffee Break #2

WHY HAVEN'T YOU HEARD FROM THE EMPLOYER?

INTERVIEWER: Well, thank you for coming in. I've enjoyed talking to you. I have a couple of other people that I need to speak with, so I should be getting back in touch with you about Wednesday.

APPLICANT: Okay, thanks. I'll be looking forward to hearing from you. Goodbye, now

On Wednesday, *you*, the applicant, sit by the phone. It doesn't ring.

What Happened?
1. MAYBE the interviewer doesn't feel that he made a definite commitment to call. He certainly didn't express himself very definitely about the whole thing.
2. MAYBE the interviewer's indefiniteness was a test to see if you would push for a more definite arrangement. You didn't.
3. MAYBE you left a wrong or illegible number and the interviewer *can't* reach you.
4. MAYBE the interviewer asked his secretary or colleague to call and she forgot or got tied up with other things.
5. MAYBE the interviewer has been out sick for the past three days.
6. MAYBE there has been an emergency in the plant (business, agency) and the interviewer hasn't had time to attend to personnel affairs.
7. MAYBE your application got lost under some papers and he can't find your phone number.

8   MAYBE he called during those "three minutes" that you were away from the phone on Wednesday

9. MAYBE he called one or more of your personal references and got no answer, so he began to lose interest in you.

10. MAYBE your phone has been working erratically and you have not received certain incoming calls, including the interviewer's

DOES IT MATTER WHY YOU HAVEN'T HEARD?
WHAT DO YOU HAVE TO LOSE? CALL BACK!

CHAPTER 10
The Application

Whether or not we are aware of it, the application process is a part of our everyday life. We "apply" for love, for membership, for marriage, and quite often for a job.

The job application is a bothersome but unavoidable part of the whole procedure of getting a job. Sometimes you fill out the application first, then present your résumé, and then go in for an interview. At other times you will present your résumé, have the interview, be hired, and only then fill out the application. The order of events will vary, but you will almost always have to fill out an application, sooner or later. (Yes, even professionals are often required to have an application on file.)

Let us point out that an application is very different from a résumé. The application is a fact sheet listing such information as address, phone number, next-of-kin, state of health, business and/or personal references, places, duration, and terms of employment, education and training, age, height, weight, and other personal or job-related information. The application form was designed to provide information for the use of employers and personnel departments. The résumé, as we pointed out earlier, is your own document, constructed by you for your own purposes. It is an advertising flyer telling good things about you to get you an interview. After it gets the interview, it has done all that it was intended to do.

Applications are kept on file along with other related personnel material, so whenever you fill one out you should always be neat and pay close attention to details. Avoid playing fast and loose with facts on an application form.

Many people lose out on jobs because they are sloppy or careless or incomplete when filling out the application. It is

---

◗ THE TRULY TARGETED RÉSUMÉ
HERE'S AN IDEA USED BY SOME VERY SHARP PRO-
FESSIONALS. THEY ARRANGE FOR AN INTERVIEW
(SOMETIMES FILLING OUT AN APPLICATION, SOME-
TIMES NOT), GO THROUGH THE INTERVIEW AND
WHEN ASKED FOR A RÉSUMÉ, CLAIM THAT THEY
FORGOT TO BRING ONE. THEY PROMISE TO GET IT
TO THE INTERVIEWER THE NEXT DAY. ACTUALLY,
ONCE THEY GET HOME, THEY REVISE THE RÉSUMÉ
TO REFLECT WHAT THEY LEARNED DURING THE
INTERVIEW. THERE IS A CERTAIN RISK IN APPEAR-
ING UNPREPARED BUT THE GAMBLE MIGHT
BE WORTH IT!

---

totally self-defeating to be haphazard about *any* phase of the job search, especially such a critical one as the application. If you're not going to do things right, why apply in the first place?

Let's pause for a moment and stop to think what happens when an employer advertises for a job and gets replies from as many as several hundred people, all of whom fill out application forms. The person who receives the applications begins immediately to separate them into three piles.

The first (and largest) pile represents those applicants who are unqualified, who apparently have spotty work records, or whose application forms are unacceptable.

The second (and smallest) pile represents those people who are going to be interviewed first. Their qualifications are all right, their work records are okay, and their applications are up to expectations—that is, neat and complete.

The third (and second-largest) pile represents the "maybes." These are the people who will be called in if the job is not filled from pile number two.

The people from pile number one are seldom granted interviews, and are almost never hired.

Consider the situation of the person who is sorting out the applications: the writing and the numerals must be clear and easy to read, because this information is generally checked. If addresses and telephone numbers are hard to decipher (or even missing), the application will automatically be passed on to pile number one (the largest). The same holds true for the rest of the information on the application. If it is missing or incomplete, or if the whole application form makes a sloppy impression . . . onto pile number one it goes!

▶ THE SCREEN-OUT

THE FIRST READING OF AN APPLICATION IS ALMOST ALWAYS A SCREENING-OUT PROCESS. IF THE FACTS DON'T HANG TOGETHER, IT'S SCREEN-OUT TIME. AND THAT MEANS NO JOB, NO MATTER HOW WELL QUALIFIED YOU MAY BE. YOU HAVE LOST BEFORE THE GAME HAS EVEN BEGUN.

The bottom line is this: if you really want a job, you'd better be sure to fill out the application form completely, neatly, and correctly. If filling out forms poses a problem for you, get a blank application and fill it out with the help of a friend. Then use it as a master application. Let it be your guide for the many other applications you will have to fill out during your job search.

On the following pages we are going to point out some of the most obvious problem areas in filling out applications. The suggestions refer to the "Application for Employment" which appears on pages 84-5. The numbers of the suggestions correspond to the numbers on the form itself.

1. NAME AND ADDRESS. Always write or (better) print neatly and legibly. Make it a work of art!
2. FILL IN *all* the information requested. If the item does not apply to you write NA (Not Applicable) or draw a neat line through the space provided. This will indicate that you have not simply overlooked the item or for some reason chosen not to answer it.
3. DON'T confuse things by listing more than one address.
4. TELEPHONE: If you have no phone, get a friend or neighbor to take messages for you. However you decide to handle it, *list a phone number.* At this preliminary stage of the game, most employers will not take the time to write you a letter.
5. EMPLOYMENT DESIRED. Always put down the specific position you are applying for. If necessary, ask for the position title. This is a key question, and if you do not answer it, you will almost certainly not be considered for employment.
6. DATE YOU CAN START. Best to put down "immediately" or "ASAP." Exact dates will age quickly.
7. SALARY DESIRED. Don't price yourself out of a job on this item, but don't sell yourself too cheaply, either. The best strategy is not to put down a particular dollar amount, but to indicate a salary *range* which, on the one hand, would be acceptable to you and, on the other hand, reflects a reasonable (usual) rate of pay for the kind of work you do. If you're really at a loss for what to say here, simply write "open" or "negotiable."

8. EDUCATION. If you have finished high school, don't bother to list your grade school.
9. FORMER EMPLOYERS. Follow instructions carefully! Be sure to begin with your present or most recent job.
10. DESCRIPTION OF WORK. Give as complete a description of your duties as you can. Start with those things that are a part of the job you are applying for.
11. REASON FOR LEAVING. If you have given information that may raise questions (dates, short-term jobs, gaps, etc.) be prepared to give reassuring answers during an interview. Never say "personal reasons," etc.
12. REFERENCES. Review the chapter on references. List phone numbers, even if they are not requested. This will make it just a little easier for the employer to process your application and contact your references. (Remember, they will call! And they will call those first who have telephone numbers on the application.)

APPLICATION FOR EMPLOYMENT
(PRE-EMPLOYMENT QUESTIONNAIRE) (AN EQUAL OPPORTUNITY EMPLOYER)

1, 2

DATE *March 16, 1986*

PERSONAL INFORMATION

NAME *Wilson   Mary   —*
LAST   FIRST   MIDDLE

SOCIAL SECURITY NUMBER *064-84-3031*

PRESENT ADDRESS **3** *237 Maple Ave.   Waterloo   Iowa*
STREET   CITY   STATE

PERMANENT ADDRESS *Same*
STREET   CITY   STATE

ARE YOU 18 YEARS OR OLDER? (*Yes*) No   **4**   PHONE NO. *(319) 861-1707*   APARTMENT NO. *—*

IN CASE OF EMERGENCY NOTIFY *Delbert Wilson   (same as applicant)*
NAME   ADDRESS   PHONE NO.

EMPLOYMENT DESIRED

5 POSITION *Clerk-Receptionist* DATE YOU CAN START *Immed.* **6** SALARY DESIRED *open*

ARE YOU EMPLOYED NOW? *No*   IF SO MAY WE INQUIRE OF YOUR PRESENT EMPLOYER? *—*

EVER APPLIED TO THIS COMPANY BEFORE? *No*   WHERE? *—*   WHEN? *—*

EVER WORKED FOR THIS COMPANY BEFORE? *No*   WHERE? *—*   WHEN? *—*

REASON FOR LEAVING *—*

NAME OF LAST SUPERVISOR AT THIS COMPANY *—*

WHO REFERRED YOU TO THIS COMPANY

[ ] EMPLOYMENT AGENCY   [ ] NEWSPAPER ADVERTISEMENT   [ ] OTHER
[ ] STATE EMPLOYMENT OFFICE   [ ] COLLEGE PLACEMENT SERVICE   [ ] WALKED IN   [X] FRIEND

EDUCATION

8 SCHOOL LEVEL	NAME AND LOCATION OF SCHOOL	*NO. OF YEARS ATTENDED?	DID YOU GRADUATE?	SUBJECTS STUDIED
GRAMMAR SCHOOL				
HIGH SCHOOL	*Barnes H.S. Ames, Iowa*	*12*	*6-'81*	*Business*
COLLEGE	*—*			
TRADE, BUSINESS OR CORRESPONDENCE SCHOOL	*Mar lake Secretarial Coll. Ames, Iowa*	*20 wks certi-ficate*	*3-'85*	*Typing office skills*

TOPS FORM 3288 (84-3)

*The Age Discrimination in Employment Act of 1967 prohibits discrimination on the basis of age with respect to individual who are at least 40 but less than 70 years of age.

LITHO IN U.S.A.

FORMER EMPLOYERS (LIST BELOW LAST THREE EMPLOYERS, STARTING WITH LAST ONE FIRST)

NAME AND ADDRESS OF PRESENT OR LAST EMPLOYER *Wingo Transport, 411 Melton St, Waterloo, Iowa*

STARTING DATE *April 1985* (MONTH / YEAR)   LEAVING DATE *July 1986* (MONTH / YEAR)

WEEKLY STARTING SALARY *$150.—*   WEEKLY FINAL SALARY *$175.—*

JOB TITLE *Office Clerk*   MAY WE CONTACT SUPERVISOR? *Yes*

NAME AND TITLE OF SUPERVISOR *Donna Bunche*   PHONE NO. *(319) 862-9662*

DESCRIPTION OF WORK *Took phone orders, maintained record of pickups & deliveries* REASON FOR LEAVING *laid off- lack of work*

NAME AND ADDRESS OF EMPLOYER *Carter Pharmaceutical Laboratories, Ames, Iowa*

STARTING DATE *9 1981* (MONTH / YEAR)   LEAVING DATE *9 1982* (MONTH / YEAR)

WEEKLY STARTING SALARY *$135.70*   WEEKLY FINAL SALARY *$146.30*

JOB TITLE *Receptionist*   MAY WE CONTACT SUPERVISOR?

NAME AND TITLE OF SUPERVISOR   PHONE NO.

DESCRIPTION OF WORK *Answer phones, make appointments, greet visitors give information* REASON FOR LEAVING *pregnant*

NAME AND ADDRESS OF EMPLOYER

STARTING DATE (MONTH / YEAR)   LEAVING DATE (MONTH / YEAR)

WEEKLY STARTING SALARY   WEEKLY FINAL SALARY

JOB TITLE   MAY WE CONTACT SUPERVISOR?

NAME AND TITLE OF SUPERVISOR   PHONE NO.

DESCRIPTION OF WORK

REASON FOR LEAVING

REFERENCES: GIVE BELOW THE NAMES OF THREE PERSONS NOT RELATED TO YOU, WHOM YOU HAVE KNOWN AT LEAST ONE YEAR.

NAME	ADDRESS	BUSINESS	YEARS ACQUAINTED
1. Alice Porter	11 Elton St., Waterloo, IA Phone 861-4401	Office Mgr.	4
2. Dan Olsoff	216 Prairie Dr., Waterloo 562-7893	Shipping Supvr	2
3. Belle Howell	27 Ryle St., Ames, IA 419-0912	Teacher	11

CHAPTER 11
The Interview

We were talking with our friend Helen the other day on the subject of job interviews. She said some interesting things that we'd like to pass along to you.

> I hate interviews! First of all, there's the hassle of getting there. I don't have a car, so I have to take a bus. Now how do they expect you to get to someplace you've never been before when you don't know where it is and you have to get there by bus? And then, once you get there, they make you wait for half an hour or so until you're good and nervous. They they take you in to talk with this important-looking person you've never even seen before, tie and everything, and he gives you a look like you were wearing a clown outfit or something. And then they get to the good part, where they really have fun picking you apart. They ask you every question they can think of to put you down. 'When did you work last? How come you left? How come you dropped out of school? Have you ever been arrested? Do you have any experience? Do you have any references we can check?' I mean, I'm sitting right there with them, and they want to call someone else to talk about me? I'll tell you, I always used to hate tests when I was in school, and these interviews are nothing but more of the same. Believe me, I *hate* interviews.

Now Helen is really a very nice woman, but sometimes we get the feeling that she goes around looking for reasons why things won't work out. It's pretty silly, and we suspect that it's an old habit she's just never broken, although she ought to. It would make life much simpler for her. But if Helen is right about only one thing it's that an interview *is* a test. And if you think back to those tests you had to take in seventh grade, you'll remember that there is only one way to pass them:

BE PREPARED!

That's it, scouts! When we said that finding a job was going to require some work we meant, among other things, a certain amount of *homework*. As you read the next section, keep in mind that the last thing you can afford at an interview is the feeling that you need to make excuses about anything: lateness; appearance; ignorance about the company; unclearness about what you have done or can do; past difficulties; shyness; lack of references . . . anything!

What are job interviews all about? The answer is simple: communication. Let's take a closer look at the communication process involved here.

Our dictionary defines the word "communication" as "an exchange of information." This means that information is both given and received by those who are communicating. Think about this with regard to your last job interview.

Were you giving useful information? How much of what you originally intended to say was lost in the process? Were you just rambling or were you really communicating?

Face-to-face communication requires that you keep your eye on a number of important factors—image, appearance, body language, speech patterns, and intonation. If you overlook something here, you might miss important cues and actually miscommunicate.

Many people regard interviews as strange and mystical ordeals that must be endured in order to achieve the final objective—a job. Nothing could be further from the truth!

◗ AN INTERVIEW IS SIMPLY A STRUCTURED SITUATION WHEN PEOPLE EXCHANGE INFORMATION —OR COMMUNICATE.

To exchange information, you must have something to say. What you convey must be carefully selected. *It is your information. Control it!*

Do not overload a potential employer with negative information relating to your personal problems or the difficulties you had on former jobs. It is not the employer's responsibility to solve your life's problems. That is your job.

Communicate only those things about yourself which are positive and relevant to the position you desire. You have gone through a period of assessment and preparation. You know who you are and what you want. Tell these things to the interviewer.

Ask questions. Is this job going to be right for you? Give positive answers. Convey information. Communicate.

Once you get the job, don't stop communicating. Keep working at it. Cultivate your skills. Keep the channels of communication open. Remember, the road to success is paved with good communications!

HOW TO SELL YOURSELF AT AN INTERVIEW

Study your own strong points and qualifications. Arrange them in your mind so you can present yourself clearly during the interview. Be prepared to discuss your past employment, salary history, and the reasons why you left previous jobs. Do not ever assume, just because you gave information about something on your résumé or on an application, that you won't have to talk about it. Remember, the employer will be trying to find out about anything that might affect your job performance. Be ready to answer as positively and directly as possible any question that may arise.

Learn as much as you can beforehand about the firm and the job. Too often job applicants go to interviews knowing absolutely nothing about what the company does or what it produces. Research!

To be thoroughly prepared for the interview you should arrive a few minutes early. Arriving too early will just give you extra time to get nervous, but never cut it so close that you risk being late! Bring along your résumé, references, letters of recommendation, and any other employment-related papers or documents you may have, but offer them only if they are asked for or if there seems to be a good opening. If you are comfortable (that is to say, prepared), your interview performance will be better.

Make a presentable appearance. Be neat and clean and dress appropriately. Appropriate dress varies somewhat, depending on the kind of job you are after. If you believe that you may be put to work immediately, dress for the job. If not, dress better than you would for work, but don't be flashy. In general, a job in which you will be dealing with the public requires a higher standard of dress.

Don't take anyone along with you to the interview. The employer is interested in hiring you, not your wife, your friend, or your child!

During the Interview

Watch your posture. Don't slouch. Try to look alert and not display signs of nervousness. If you tend to fidget, fold your hands.

Do your utmost to answer all questions as accurately and honestly as possible. Giving the interviewer complete and satisfying answers is often the key to being hired. Whenever you have an opportunity, emphasize your strong points and the accomplishments that make you especially qualified for the job in question.

Listen carefully to what you are being asked. If a question seems vague, politely ask the interviewer to clarify it.

At all times, show proper respect for the person interviewing you. Do not smoke, chew gum, or try to get buddy-buddy. Remember, this is not your "turf."

Speak with confidence and enthusiasm. It is best not to bluff or exaggerate, but if you do, make sure you can deliver the goods.

Whatever you do or say, *don't talk too much*.

Don't mention your personal, domestic, or financial troubles. You are there to fill the *employer's* needs. How you fill your own needs is *your* responsibility and is not a topic to be brought up in a job interview.

Don't ask about job benefits until you are actually offered the job.

Be certain that you like the job you are applying for and that you are actually capable of doing it. If you accept a job you can't really do or don't genuinely enjoy, the odds are pretty good that you won't keep it. And if you don't, it will simply be that much harder to get the next one.

Regardless of the outcome, smile, say "Thank you!" and end the interview on a positive, friendly note. Maybe you didn't get the job, but you did make a contact!

AFTER THE INTERVIEW

Write down as much as you can remember of what the interviewer said or asked and all the answers and comments you made in reply. (Never take notes *during* the interview.) Even if you don't get the job, you can learn something for the next interview. Or . . . you can always try again on this one.

Finally, write and send a "thank you" note as soon as you get back from the interview.

See the Appendix for an example of a thank-you note.

▶ WHY A "THANK YOU" NOTE?
THIS IS AN OPPORTUNITY TO MAKE THE EMPLOYER
THINK WELL OF YOU. IT IS THE POLITE THING TO
DO, IT GIVES YOU THE CHANCE TO COMMENT ON
ANYTHING YOU MAY HAVE FORGOTTEN TO SAY
DURING THE INTERVIEW, AND ALL IT COSTS IS THE
PRICE OF A POSTAGE STAMP.

INTERVIEW CHECKLIST

☐ Am I in the right frame of mind to look for a job?

☐ Am I dressed appropriately?

☐ Have I done my homework? Do I know enough about the company?

☐ Am I really prepared? Do I have an updated résumé or fact sheet? Are my references available for contact, and have they been informed that they may be receiving calls about me?

☐ Am I ready for the difficult questions I may be asked?

☐ Am I ready to ask questions of my own?

☐ Do I have my social security card with me?

☐ Will I need any other documents such as a draft card, licenses, union cards, etc.?

☐ Have I properly planned my time? Will I be able to arrive a few minutes early? Is my schedule free in case the interview runs late?

☐ Am I prepared to leave a positive impression with the interviewer regardless of the outcome?

☐ Do I really want the job if it is offered to me?

CHAPTER 12
Follow-up

After sending the "thank you" note, don't let the job lead wither and die on the vine. Most people who are interviewed and not hired right away never let the employer know that they are still interested. Stop and think about this. It is quite possible that the job may never have been filled. Sometimes employers decide to wait a week, two weeks, a month before actually hiring someone.

Even if someone was hired, he or she may not have stayed in the position. Most of the things that can go wrong are likely to do so during the first two weeks. Begin your follow-up campaign two weeks after your interview by sending a letter expressing your continued interest in the position and letting the employer know that you are still available. The letter also enables you to establish communications on a more friendly basis with the person who interviewed you. It could pay off later. In your follow-up letter, you might mention that you are still impressed with the company and the scope of their operations.

♦ THE WHY AND THE WHY-NOT
WHY GO TO ALL THE TROUBLE OF A FOLLOW-UP CAMPAIGN WHEN THE COMPANY WOULDN'T HIRE YOU IN THE FIRST PLACE? IF YOU WERE REALLY INTERESTED IN THE COMPANY BEFORE, AND IF A FOLLOW-UP CAMPAIGN MIGHT GET YOU A SECOND SHOT . . . THEN, WHY NOT?

A few days after sending out your follow-up letter, call the person who interviewed you and ask, in a friendly manner, whether he/she got your letter and whether you may come in for another interview. If the answer is "No," then ask to be kept in mind for future openings and inquire whether there is a possibility of your being referred to someone else. Impress upon the person who interviewed you that you are a determined, qualified person who deserves to get a job in the field even though there are no openings at this particular company.

◗ ANY APPLICATION OR RÉSUMÉ WHICH WAS SUBMITTED MORE THAN SIX MONTHS AGO SHOULD BE RESUBMITTED.

To upgrade your follow-up contacts with "second-time-around" job leads, continue to build up your information bank through various media, annual reports, and word-of-mouth.
For example:
1. Personnel changes through promotion, transfer, or death. (Talk with company employees or even read the obituaries.)
2. News that federal, state, or municipal contracts have been awarded.
3. News of expansion at either the corporate or local level.
4. Advertising changes which suggest new approaches or introduce new products.

Use this and any other information as the basis for a fresh approach to your follow-up campaign. Remember, a key feature of the campaign is the backtracking and double-checking system you apply to all those places where you had job interviews.

Let us assume that you had 20 interviews in January. If you are following our plan, you should have reworked all of these job contacts by the middle of February.

Your next step is to apply the same strategy each following month. Even though this requires work and entails detailed and extensive recordkeeping, it will pay off.

Here's how your records might look:

> Sept. 19 . . . . . Phone call, interview appointment
> Sept. 23 . . . . . Interviewed by R. Simmons, pending
> Sept. 24 . . . . . Thank-you note sent to Simmons

Sept. 29 . . . . . Called Simmons, job given to
someone else

Oct. 13 . . . . . Sent letter to Simmons men-
tioning recent award of gov't
contract to his company

Oct. 20 . . . . . Called Simmons, new interview
on Oct. 23

Oct. 23 . . . . . No openings with Simmons, referred to Ledco Inc., Mr. Wu

Many people who are in hiring positions appreciate and are impressed by applicants who are persistent. Eventually, they may hire you for that very reason—you refuse to take no for an answer. They will assume that you have "something special" that will make you successful on the job. Or, they may be happy to refer you to another company.

Remember that being assertive and persistent does not mean being pushy or annoying. Showing an interest in a company and trying to fill their employment need is what a job search is all about. Keep the doors open. Once you slam them shut, it's hard to walk through them again.

CHAPTER 13

Daily Plan

A "Daily Job Plan" can help you get organized.

Let's once again face the facts. If we can trust the statistics, the average working person might have up to twenty jobs during his/her working life which is an average of 45 years. This means that job hunting is something that you will do several more times during your life.

Why not get organized? It's just one more way to simplify getting the job.

The Daily Job Plan is a tool and you can use it in any way you choose. Use the chart on the next page as a guide to create your own daily plan sheet. But do something. Otherwise, you'll mess up your own plan. And your plan is to get a job, right?

◗ THE SIMPLEST DEFINITION OF "PLAN" IS "TO ARRANGE BEFOREHAND." (TO PUT IT ANOTHER WAY: YOU HAVE TO PLAN TO PLAN!)

DAILY JOB PLAN

Day _____

Who am I Contacting Today?

Name	Phone No. or Address	How Contacted? (In Person or Letter)	What Happened?

Carryovers to Contact Tomorrow:

Name	Phone No. or Address	How Contacted

My Scores for Today

Phone Calls	By Mail	In Person	Inter-view

Comments: _____

_____

_____

CHAPTER 14

Your New Job and How to Keep It

If you have taken our advice seriously and have followed our suggestions (the appropriate ones), you should be hot on the trail of a job by now. Maybe you've already found one.

If you haven't worked recently—and even if you have—there are things you should think about before starting a new job.

Is this really the right job for you?

Remember what we said about attitude? If you aren't convinced that you genuinely *want* to do this work, you probably won't be doing it for very long. We are not trying to pass judgment, but in our profession, we have seen it happen too often: people who take jobs they don't really want either tire of them quickly and quit, or they do a lousy job and get fired.

Don't accept the first job that comes along unless it's right for you. If your ideal job is out of the question right now—perhaps you need more schooling or training, maybe there have been a lot of layoffs in your field, or the job requires experience that you just don't have yet—you may have to settle for second or third best *for now*.

If this is the case, make a plan! Find out what you need to do to get what you want. Then start off with the things you can do right *now*. This way you will know that your present job (or the job you are soon to have) is just a first step toward something much better. Give it your best whether the job deserves it or not. You deserve it! In this way you will be coming closer to what you are really after, namely, the best.

◗ YOU CAN'T BUILD A REPUTATION ON WHAT YOU'RE GOING TO DO.

Be aware that when you accept a job, you are making a commitment to do your best for the employer. Most employers watch new employees very carefully. They know from experience that people tend to slack off after a while. If an employee's performance is barely adequate from the start, the boss will begin to look for ways to get rid of the person.

Many people begin the process of losing their jobs the moment they get them. Often, they don't realize that the daily job commitment requires just as much discipline and effort as the job search did. From the start, they take their jobs for granted.

In many respects a successful job search can be compared to a courtship which has led to marriage. Smiles come easily, and people in the company are agreeable and receptive. You can be ambitious, and your lofty goals seem within reach. You seek to please the object of your desires, and even promise loyalty in phrases such as "a career position with your company."

Once the "knot" has been tied and the job offer accepted, a brief honeymoon follows. How sweet it is! But we all know what it means when "the honeymoon is over."

People often allow their level of productivity to drop even before they are firmly established in a new position. What a waste of all the energy they expended on the job search! What a shame to fall back into old ways and abandon the good habits one has developed. How easy it is to forget that what didn't work in the past will almost certainly not work now.

It is a serious error to think, once the ball is rolling, that it will continue to do so by itself. There is no such thing as just coasting!

A common, but self-defeating attitude is reflected in statements such as "It's just a job." Do you remember the conversation between Henry and Arlene? The "just-a-job" attitude leaves no room for the positive feelings, goals and ambition we need to produce changes in our lives. It is true only when short-term or temporary positions are involved. Otherwise it hides both our goals and the reasons we had for accepting a given position in the first place. Whatever these reasons were, we must be clear about them.

What is our advice to new employees?

Make the job your own. Make the job fit you. Now is the

time to think in terms of growth and development. Learn all there is to know about your new job and how you can do it even better. Grow into the job, search out its core and ask yourself how you can become what you really want to be.

If you find out that your present position is not going to satisfy you in the long run, ask yourself what you can gain from it that will profit you in the future. New beginnings are a time to take a close look at things. The challenge is there. Accept it!

Here are some specific issues to keep in mind during your first months on a new job:

- Don't miss time and don't be late. This is the single largest reason for the firing of newly hired workers.
- Try to learn from your fellow employees, but don't pick up their bad habits. They aren't being watched as closely as you are. Just because Sally or Joe always takes an extra long break doesn't mean that it's okay for you to do so.
- Don't argue when you're given instructions. You may in fact know better, but most bosses don't like "know-it-alls." Just perform your duties as instructed.
- If you think you're being picked on or discriminated against, you may be right, particularly if you are a member of a minority at the place of work. Don't let a creep force you out. If you quit (or blow up), the bad guys win. Hang on until you have another job to go to. Otherwise you'll be right back where you started.
- Keep working on getting along with others. If your boss and your co-workers like you, you're ahead of the game, and getting ahead is the name of the game.
- Keep your eyes open and learn all you can. You probably won't have this job forever. Increase your skills, make yourself valuable. Some people resent being asked to do work which lies outside of their "job description." Others see this as an opportunity. Be the second kind—for your own good.
- One final word of advice. If you have ever had problems with a job before, stop right now and try to understand how these problems came about. Figure out what you can do so that you will not come up against the same problems at your present job site or at some time in the future. Try to learn from past mistakes.

104 / THE HIDDEN JOB MARKET

The ins and outs of finding work are innumerable. We could go on for many volumes, and the thought of writing a sequel to this book is already under discussion.

Thousands of people have come to us with their questions, and in just a few pages we have tried to distill all the advice we passed along to them.

If you follow our advice, you will soon be among the numerous individuals who can point to the benefits they have reaped. You'll soon have the job you always wanted. Maybe you'll even land a better job than you ever dreamed of. Others have succeeded. Why shouldn't you?

CHAPTER 15

Getting a Job in The Future

Since the first, smaller edition of *Secrets of The Hidden Job Market* was self-published in 1982, we have received many letters from readers asking for our advice about getting a job. We have attempted to answer all of them as best we could in a page or two. One of the most intriguing inquiries was the following. (As you will see, we felt this letter deserved an answer in great detail.)

Dear Secrets:

What is it going to be like by the year 2000; how will jobs be obtained then? What is going to be different? What is going to be the same?

Afraid for the future!

Dear Afraid:

PREDICTION #1: THE HIDDEN JOB MARKET WILL BE EVEN MORE HIDDEN!

So-called "advances" in electronic communications and related technology will make it more difficult to find out where the jobs are, because it will be more difficult to get to the people who have the power to hire you. There will be more answering machines (or telecommunication information machines, if you will) and bosses and managers will be harder to contact. Even today, the trend is toward hiring fewer people and employing more machines to do the work.

Today, public media is often owned and managed by "distant" executives. Absentee ownership by large newspaper syndicates or conglomerates leads to lessened involvement in the community where the newspaper or radio/TV station is located.

Classified advertising has been on the decline for decades. With less involved ownership, this trend will continue, simply because display advertising is more profitable, cost-effective, and correspondingly less personal. The help-wanted ads will not completely disappear but their value to the jobseeker will greatly diminish: there will be fewer of them, and small to mid-size employers will find the cost for advertising beyond their means.

These employers will rely more and more on their own networks to supply them with new employees. Formerly visible jobs will thus become a part of the Hidden Job Market.

PREDICTION #2: STATE-RUN EMPLOYMENT SERVICES WILL CLOSE DOWN!

Many state-operated job service agencies have been funded by federal monies for the past 30 years. Now with the current drive toward cutbacks and accountability, many of their services are being drastically curtailed. The truth of the matter is (and nobody wants to say this!) that the majority of the state employment agencies were operating with 50-year-old ideas and were simply not doing their jobs. Over the years, they have been wasting taxpayers' money and jobseekers' time. Ironically, in many areas, when state-employed "employment counselors" were laid off, they floundered because they did not know how to get jobs!

If they did nothing else (and many of them did next to nothing!) the state job services at least collected information on job openings. Their ability to make this information available to the jobseeker was often questionable, but those individuals who were persistent and demanding enough could usually make good use of such information.

In any event, by the year 2000 (or earlier), the state job services will no longer be a resource for jobseekers.

PREDICTION #3: PRIVATE EMPLOYMENT AGENCIES WILL CHANGE

Employment agencies have been in a process of change for the past several years. For instance, small agencies have all but disappeared in many areas. Generally, these small agencies were staffed by home-grown people who knew the local labor market.

Increasingly, these small agencies are being replaced by large, centralized job agencies, depersonalization, less responsiveness to individual demands, more corporate thinking and less creative thinking.

Remember that, at present, employment agencies do not find jobs for people, but seek to fill the requirements of employers. The future will not only bring more of the same, but employment agencies will cease to handle the lower-level jobs. They will gear themselves more to the management and professional levels, staying away from semi-professional (technical) and entry-level positions.

This shift in focus will be accompanied by a new style of presenting potential employees to employers. Video films have already been utilized to a limited degree (and with success) by jobseekers, but increased availability of equipment and lowering of prices will increase the use of this method. As video presentations are used more and more (as a kind of live, in-color, talking-head résumé), employers will come to accept and even expect the submission of such videos.

A logical extension of this method of presentation will be a computer-video hook-up from city to city (or from office to office) where the job applicant will appear on camera and will actually be interviewed by an employer from a remote location. This interviewing method will require that the job applicant be better trained in communication and self-presentation.

For the jobseeker of the future, this simply means that to get the jobs which pay more money, an individual must pay more money up-front for preparation.

If the state job services and private employment agencies are not going to be available to help the entry-level worker of the future, who *is* going to help them?

The same people and organizations who are currently providing the most help to people looking for entry-level jobs will continue to provide even more help in the future.

Schools   Colleges, universities, and high schools have become increasingly aware of the need for more programs and courses in sharpening job-seeking skills. Proprietary

schools such as truck driver training, secretarial training, medical-legal clerical training, are putting more
and more emphasis on placement and how to get a
job.

Libraries   In addition to the job information centers already
available at many libraries, in the future libraries will
become more involved in sponsoring job clubs,
workshops relating to jobseeking, and seminars for
employers and jobseekers.

Human   The various government-funded programs (i.e., JTPA)
Services   will offer special assistance for those persons seeking
Agencies   entry-level positions.

PREDICTION #4:
THE USE OF RESUMES WILL CHANGE

By the year 2000, nearly all employers will demand résumés
for all types of jobs. Even for the simplest entry-level jobs, all
applicants will have to submit a résumé, regardless of their
educational level. More and more businesses are adding word
processing systems to their operations, and nearly all schools
have added (or soon will add) computer literacy courses to their
curriculums. Employers will feel justified in assuming that most
people have the ability (and access to equipment) to prepare a
résumé.

Given the ease with which a word processing system can turn
a time-consuming writing project into a relatively quick and
simple one, employers will probably demand more and more
detail in the résumés of tomorrow. When one considers the
stringency with which EEO, Human Rights, and other watchdog
commissions are working to safeguard individual privacy, it
seems likely that employers will use the résumé to ask the
questions they can't legally ask during an interview. This means
that personal information such as age, weight, height, marital
status, state of health, number of children and home ownership
will become required information on résumés.

The résumé of the future will become more of a historical
document and less of a sales tool. The more concrete a résumé is,
the better. Chronology will receive greater emphasis and the

ideal résumé will probably be chronological with each position meticulously detailed according to functions performed.

In the future, jobseekers would be advised to have their résumés typed (or word processed) by a competent specialist. In an age when instant communication becomes matter-of-fact, mistakes in syntax, grammar and typing become glaringly obvious and will end further consideration of a job candidate. For any job!

PREDICTION #5: REFERENCES AND LETTERS OF RECOMMENDATION WILL BECOME LESS IMPORTANT

Employers will increasingly realize that references and letters of recommendation are a carryover from the Victorian period and that they have little value in today's fast-changing world. References and recommendations are highly subjective. Rarely does the writer of a recommendation give an "honest" assessment of the applicant. Instead, most recommendations include only positive statements about a job applicant. They do not address the issue of competency; only the employer can really perceive whether that particular person will succeed at that particular job.

The hiring process of the future will rely more on technology and less on another person's word. The lie detector (though so controversial right now) will be improved and put to greater use than ever before. Wherever money actually changes hands, lie detectors will be used to gauge honesty.

Their real value for employers will be in the pre-employment process. Applicants will be asked about possible substance abuse, reliability, honesty, and will be asked to verify certain facts in the application. Skill and competency tests will also be used more frequently, and in a wider variety of applications. Math, literacy, typing, and driving tests are widely used today. These tests will be joined by a range of specific performance-rating exercises designed to assess a person's ability to do a specific job or demonstrate a particular skill, as well as for common sense, teamwork, carefulness, and other desirable qualities.

Presently, civil rights statutes guard against discriminatory pre-employment testing. In the future, when it becomes a matter of saving money (i.e., reducing insurance premiums), the civil rights of individuals may be put aside. At least, it will be much more difficult to lie or bluff successfully when applying for a job. It will be more essential than ever to *acquire solid skills* and to *keep your record clean.*

PREDICTION #6: JOB HUNTING
WILL BECOME MORE FREQUENT

The idea of getting a job and staying with it for a lifetime is no longer a part of the American Dream. This idea has been replaced by the voracious demands of the age of instant gratification and goes the way of the one-car, one-home, one-marriage, way of life.

If there is more absentee ownership of homes and businesses, less local involvement of banking, insurance, and media, people will feel less and less of a tie to their hometowns and will be more transient. More people will change jobs more quickly than before; Americans will move faster, and more often, to where the jobs are. This phenomenon will directly affect the economy and will change existing businesses or create new businesses.

In the future, the Hidden Job Market will become an even more viable approach. As more and more Americans handle jobseeking like a game of musical chairs, the people who are aware of the Hidden Job Market are going to be among the winners of the game and have a seat to sit on while many other people are standing in the unemployment lines.

PREDICTION #7: THE UNEMPLOYMENT
RATE WILL RISE!

Many factors will contribute to the rise of the unemployment rate.

One factor is simply that jobs of all kinds will be harder to get. The hardest jobs to get will be at the sub-professional or mid-management level or at the technician level. These mid-level jobs will be caught in an economic squeeze. An increase in the minimum wage will drain off money and force businesses to cut elsewhere: sub-professional, mid-management, technician. And upper management will demand (and get) more out of retirement due to higher federal tax rates on individual savings toward retirement.

Another major factor in the rise in unemployment is an appalling lack of planning to meet the needs of a service-oriented economy. The federal government, the educational systems, the labor unions, and big business are all to blame for this failure. The state governments are also contributing to this future mess by taking a head-in-the-sand attitude and waiting for miracles to happen.

Simply put, the situation is this: if the United States continues to become more of a service-oriented economy and the workers are not trained for service-oriented jobs, there will be more unemployed persons. As it stands now, the majority of training programs in this country train people to run machines. Not enough people are being trained to fix the machines.

PREDICTION #8: BY THE YEAR 2000 THE DEMAND FOR CERTAIN JOBS WILL INCREASE SIGNIFICANTLY

This is always an interesting area to consider. Where will these jobs be?

The health-care field, medicine: Every type of health-care worker, from doctors and technicians to nurses and hospital aides, will be in great demand. Why? Americans will become even more health-conscious and will live longer because of it.

Service workers: This category covers everything from waiters, bartenders, janitors, housekeeping personnel, to dishwashers, stock clerks, counterpeople, etc. These jobs demand few specialized skills and, in many instances, these skills can be transferred from one job to another.

Protective service workers: Police personnel, firefighters, personal security people, guards, marshals, crossing guards, prison guards. Society's need for security and the individual's need for protection has made this an area in which the need for workers is doubling and tripling.

Computer services: Operators, programmers, repair people, salespeople, service technicians, customer service workers. Everything related to computers (with the exception of computer manufacture) has created a demand for more workers. This demand will peak and level off. By the year 2000 it will show a slow and steady decline.

The greatest need will be for clerical workers of all kinds; the smallest need will be for farmers and farm workers. This has been true for the last twenty years and will continue for at least the next twenty.

The chart on the next page shows the percent of change projected for the major occupational groups.

OTHER PREDICTIONS

For most Americans, work means a car, a home, entertainment, vacations, money, education, retirement income, and a way to ensure ongoing fun and leisure. If today's job is only a means of obtaining material possessions, fun and leisure time, and if work itself has no intrinsic value for the worker, then the future of productivity and the true meaning of work are in great jeopardy.

Most people over 40 who have achieved certain career goals agree that if all the various benefits of employment were to be considered (pay, position, work environment, fringe benefits), the most important factor to them would be job satisfaction. This means that rather than getting more money, fringe benefits, or other considerations, most career workers over 40 would rather be happy on the job.

The future service-oriented economy has already been characterized by some job experts as 21st-century sweatshops. This unhappy image doesn't conjure up a rosy future for the average entry-level worker.

Predicting a rosy future seems to be an occupational hazard for many writers who specialize in employment-related matters. A syndicated newspaper column recently predicted that, by the year 2000, there would be 66,000 more jobs in an upstate New

PERCENT CHANGE IN EMPLOYMENT BY MAJOR OCCUPATIONAL GROUP

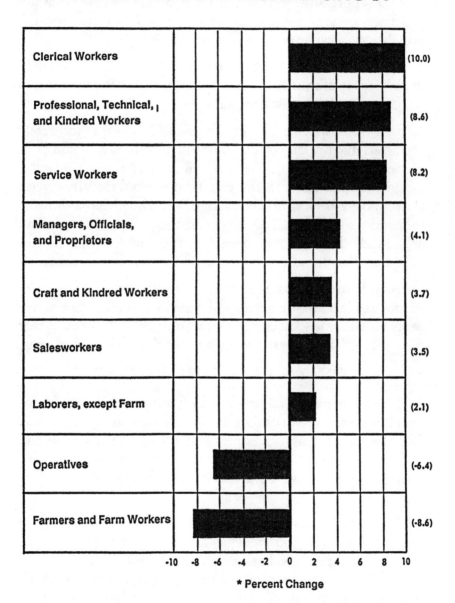

Occupational Group	Percent Change
Clerical Workers	(10.0)
Professional, Technical, and Kindred Workers	(8.6)
Service Workers	(8.2)
Managers, Officials, and Proprietors	(4.1)
Craft and Kindred Workers	(3.7)
Salesworkers	(3.5)
Laborers, except Farm	(2.1)
Operatives	(-6.4)
Farmers and Farm Workers	(-8.6)

-10 -8 -6 -4 -2 0 2 4 6 8 10

* Percent Change

York metropolitan area. The area mentioned had in 1986 a working force of 400,000; this would mean a 17.7% increase in the number of available jobs. However, in the same paper another report lamented the declining population in the area and still another article in the same paper pointed out that the population of older persons was steadily increasing.

If all these facts are indeed true (and they may well be) then the jobseeker of the future should be aware that the times could be, if not tough, at least confusing.

In a book written as recently as 1982, it was inaccurately predicted that the largest job growth geographically would be in the Southwest and on the Eastern Seaboard. Actually, the largest job growth has been in the eastern metropolitan areas, with Boston, New York City, Long Island, and Philadelphia showing tremendous increases. This is because these major metropolitan areas (and others, too) are rebuilding their business and residential areas. This trend will continue on into the 21st century.

All job forecasters agree on two issues: first, that the majority of jobs available in the future will depend upon (but not necessarily be in) the field of computer technology, and secondly, that these jobs will be in the service area rather than in manufacturing.

WHAT IS THE FUTURE FOR YOU?

It's easy to make predictions about the future for millions of people; you are never completely right, never completely wrong. You play the percentages. Some of what you say will be true and some of it won't. It really doesn't matter a lot, because your predictions will have no effect on the futures of individual jobseekers.

Most adults who are looking for work, or who are in the process of changing jobs, will pay little attention to prognostications, and rightly so. What happens in the next fifteen years will have little visible direct affect on most people, nor is there much they can do to change what happens. Nevertheless, it is reassuring and occasionally useful to know what is likely to happen in the future.

For instance, if you are presently working in the manufacturing area and you read a prediction that there will be 15% fewer jobs in manufacturing by the year 2000, what do you do?

Ask questions. How old are you now? If you are going to retire in 10 years, this probably won't affect you at all.

What kind of job do you presently have? If manufacturing in your geographical area is being phased out, which jobs will be the last to go? Can you do the same job somewhere else (i.e., in service or non-manufacturing areas)?

By the year 2000, how many workers will actually be needed to maintain a full work force in manufacturing? If the present work force is reduced by 15% or more through natural attrition (death, retirement, resignation) and if nobody new is hired, then there will be no actual job loss.

Our bottom-line recommendation is this: read books (this one and others) and newspapers (front page and business page). Talk to people at work and elsewhere. Keep in touch with what is going on, but take it all with many grains of salt. At the same time, think about what you would do *if!*—if your employer went bankrupt, if your plant relocated, if your job were phased out.

Keep learning and keep thinking. Your career begins and ends with you.

To help you in thinking about your own career and your own future, we are including here a number of other readers' letters which address issues we feel to be of general interest. Remember: any employee may one day be a jobseeker.

Dear Secrets:

After a ten-year stint as a homemaker, I am planning to go back to work. Although I was successful in my field (legal secretary) before leaving to raise a family, I find I'm just not in the swing of it anymore.

Career Changer

Dear Career Changer:

For a woman in your position self-assessment is essential. What employers are concerned with is: can you do the job or not? Sounds obvious? Well, it is, but take a careful look to see just how you measure up in this respect. The question is one of competency. You may have typed 65 words per minute in 1976, but can you still do it now? What kind of word processor did you use ten years ago? Are you abreast of what has been happening in that area over the last ten years? Take a good look at your skills and consider brushing them up. This will give you an underlying feeling of security when you approach employers. They will sense your self-confidence and feel better about giving you the chance you need to get back into the work force. Many temporary employment agencies can provide not only an assessment of your current skill level, but also brush-up courses and short-term work assignments to ease you back into the field.

Another tool for easing the re-entry process is the functional résumé. Rather than emphasizing dates as conventional, chronological résumés do, a functional résumé will stress your capabilities and downplay that gap in your employment history. There is absolutely no shame in withdrawing from the 9-to-5 world and raising a family. You can be proud of what you've done with your time.

Dear Secrets:

If I were to write down all the experience I've had and try to put it into résumé form it would probably run three, four, maybe even five pages. Where does one draw the line? Sometimes I feel as though I could even write a short novel about the jobs I've had.

Writer

Dear Writer:

As far as the novel is concerned, try a writer's workshop. Good luck, it can be lucrative! But as far as résumés are concerned don't even think about anything over two pages.

A résumé is like a personal advertisement. It doesn't have to include everything you've ever done—it just has to sell you by including the relevant information. Keep in mind the primary purpose of a résumé. It won't get you a job, but it *can* get you an interview. There will be time to touch on many important issues when you are talking with the employer face to face. Make it easy on the employer, keep it short and sweet. Excuse the platitude, but quantity doesn't mean quality. You have somewhere between 30 seconds and a minute of the employer's reading time. It's got to be a fast pitch.

Dear Secrets:

People have repeatedly told me to write a thank-you note after a job interview—even when I have not been offered work. I can't begin to tell you how this goes against my grain. What am I supposed to say, "Thanks for wrecking my day!"? What's the use?

Irked

Dear Irked:

Not only should you send a thank-you, you should take steps not to let a job lead die on the vine. The majority of people never return after being interviewed and not being hired.

There are no guarantees that the newly hired person will work out, or that the job was even filled. Sometimes, for one reason or another, the job is not filled and is left on the back burner for a time.

Even if someone was hired, there are many reasons why they may not have stayed in the position. And most of the things that can go wrong are likely to do so during the first few weeks.

Begin your follow-up campaign two or three weeks after your interview by first sending a letter expressing your continued interest in the position and letting the employer know that you are still available. This also becomes your opportunity to establish a more friendly connection with the person who interviewed you. It could pay off later.

I hate to wreck your day by giving you even more "bad news" from the desk of the employment consultant but a thank-you note is only the first step in an ongoing communications process with potential employers, and that includes those who may already have turned you down.

If you're really serious about landing a job, you can't afford to neglect a single contact—ever.

Dear Secrets:

Do you think that it's worth the effort to respond to those little two-or-three-line ads in the classified section, the ones that just say to send a résumé and salary requirements to such-and-such a box number?

Undecided

Dear Undecided:

Theoretically, any job lead is worth following up unless it involves an undue financial outlay or an inordinate amount of your time or energy. I would, however, definitely not pin my hopes on the kind of ads you describe. In the employment biz they're called "blind" ads. Sometimes they're not even based on genuine job openings.

Consider the following example. A large New York City-based accounting firm is planning to open new offices the following year. The VP in charge of the project needs to gather information on the availability and financial expectations of the clerical and professional staff she requires, and therefore places one of those two-or-three-line ads in the classified section.

It is, I feel, safe to say that she reads the 100-120 résumés people have submitted with interest, perhaps even with gratitude. But it never enters her mind to make a job offer. There is still plenty of time for that when springtime comes!

Dear Secrets:

About six weeks ago, I was laid off from a position I've had for 2½ years. Now that I have taken care of some things I had always been wanting to do (but couldn't ever find time for) the fact that I am unemployed is becoming very real to me. I'm actively looking for work but wonder whether anyone has ever computed the average amount of time people spend between jobs. It would be a comfort to know just where I stand in relation to the mean.

Inquirer

Dear Inquirer:

I am aware that statistics have a certain appeal. The average time between jobs is 12 weeks (84 days). But beware, you're on thin ice! You are, I fear, about to fall into what we call the "statistical trap."

This is not the place to discuss the shortcomings of various measures of central tendency. My question is: what good is it to compare your job search efforts with those of some abstract statistic a government agency has published?

Let's take national, state, and local unemployment rates as a further example of how statistics can be misused.

When the unemployment rate is high, people tend to take comfort in the fact that a lot of other folks are out of work too. When the rate is low, people feel especially miserable about being unemployed and can find no solace in the statistics.

We prefer to talk about personal statistics. If you've been laid off, your personal unemployment rate is 100%. That's outrageously high! If you are employed, your unemployment rate is 0%, which is ideal. Statistics can be fun but they tend to distract jobseekers from the real issues. If you need to find work now, then make a genuine commitment to finding it as soon as you can. If you want to dawdle, there's little anyone can do to stop you. Either way, simply make up your mind—the choice is yours.

Dear Secrets:

I've heard that one of the best ways of finding work is by contacting other people. My difficulty is that I don't know where to begin. Who should I actually be contacting?

Uncertain

Dear Uncertain:

There is no doubt that the process of talking to people will produce more jobs than any other approach. It's called networking.

The subject is virtually inexhaustible but try this for openers. Draw up a list of *everyone* you know, that's right—everyone, even individuals who are not working. For example, the immediate family, relatives, friends, neighbors, roommates, former co-workers, former classmates, teachers, clergymen, partygoers, fellow players or sportsmen, church members, etc.

Contact each person on your list. Tell each one what you are looking for. Give each a copy of your résumé. Ask each for advice and assistance. Stay in touch with your contacts and let them know you are still looking. Fully 48% of all employment is obtained through networking. That's just about every other job! Need I say more?

Dear Secrets:

Is there any way of deducting at least some of the expenses involved in the job search from one's income taxes? It seems like there ought to be.

Hopeful

Dear Hopeful:

Indeed, there is. In the past the IRS has made allowances for résumé preparation, mailing copies of the résumé to prospective employers, traveling expenses for job search-related trips, and even part of the cost of moving to a new location.

Some of the items are subject to dollar limits, and many of these tax-deduction techniques require that you start implementing them right away, i.e., before the end of the year. Start saving your receipts now for deductions you will list on your next year's tax return.

For exact and up-to-date information contact the IRS. As we all know, they have the final say. Their publications are free (ask for publication #17) and so is the phone call: 1 (800) 424-3676. Sometimes it takes quite a while to get through, so be prepared to wait. But, after all, patience is a virtue, isn't it?

Dear Secrets:

I am well aware of the fact that a résumé should never be submitted without a cover letter. But everyone has different ideas as to what should be included in such a letter. Are there any general guidelines? I have about three ads to answer and I don't want to postpone sending the résumés off too much longer.

Hurried

Dear Hurried:

Yes, there are guidelines, and they are relatively simple. If you were able to write to us here and express your question clearly, you ought to be able to manage a cover letter.

In paragraph #1, explain why you are writing the letter. Are you responding to an ad, did someone refer you, or did you get the name of the company and the Vice-President from a directory or other source? State as specifically as possible what position you are applying for or inquiring about.

In paragraph #2, state why you are interested in *this* company. Show that you have taken the time to find out who they are and what they do. Explain *briefly* what contributions you can make to the operation and what qualifications, experience, or personal qualities will enable you to be a productive and valuable employee. Be specific, and above all, be positive. Avoid such phrases as "although I have never worked in this field . . ."

In paragraph #3, note that you are enclosing a résumé. Express a desire to meet, in the near future, the person to whom you are writing. If you wish, suggest a possible day or days which would be convenient for you. Indicate that you hope to be contacted by a specific date and that you will call if you have heard nothing by then.

And, please, keep it to one page.

Dear Secrets:

Last week I had an interview for a technical position in which I am genuinely interested. The woman who was offering the job told me in no uncertain terms that she liked my credentials and that I would be given very serious consideration.

I felt like I had landed the job and was really enthusiastic about it. She said she would be in touch with me the following Tuesday. Well, Tuesday came, and Tuesday went, but the phone didn't ring. I'm in a quandary as to whether I should call back and see what's up or not. Would that be pushy of me?

Cautious

Dear Cautious:

BY ALL MEANS, CALL BACK! Don't wait another minute. You are right to be cautious because you don't want to crowd someone who is (hopefully) involved in the process of making a decision in your favor. On the other hand, you don't want to let the person off the hook too easily. You have a life to lead. You have a valid and very real objective: you must get a job.

One way of handling the situation in a non-threatening manner is to call this woman up and say that although you had been looking forward to hearing from her last Tuesday, you were forced to step out for a few minutes and were afraid you might have missed her call. That puts the ball squarely in her court.

In the future do not hesitate to call back. Consider all the things which might have happened to prevent an employer from contacting you as arranged.

Here are a few things that might explain such an irregularity:

Maybe the interviewer asked a secretary or colleague to call you and that person forgot or got tied up with other things.

Maybe there was an emergency at the business and the interviewer simply hasn't had time to attend to anything else.

Maybe the phone has been working erratically and you have not received certain incoming calls.

Maybe the interviewer called during those three minutes you were actually away from the phone.

Or would you prefer to go on wondering?

Dear Secrets

Here's a simple, straightforward question for you: How many references should you list on a résumé?

Wonderer

Dear Wonderer:

Here's a simple answer: Zero! I think what is complicating matters is the final entry, that last line on many résumés which frequently reads *References furnished upon request* or words to that effect. This is correct procedure; including references on the same sheet is not.

Generally, three to five references will suffice. A lot can be said on the subject of references, but one thing stands out as being absolutely essential. References must be available for contact. Even the best references will do you no good if potential employers cannot reach them, and reach them during business hours at that. Many people take work home with them at night, but very few people enjoy it. If at all possible, make your references the ones that are easily accessible during the day. If you cause an employer extra work even before you are hired, it will not reflect well on you. Make yourself as easy to hire as possible.

Dear Secrets

I realize that this might be asking a bit much, and I am aware of the danger of oversimplification, but what is the single most important factor involved in a job search?

Short 'n' Sweet

Dear Short 'n' Sweet:

I am tempted to respond to your question with the short (and singularly unhelpful!) answer it merits! While we're at it, wouldn't you also like me to tell you what the best job in the world is, or perhaps the name and address of the world's best employer?

Seriously, now, a job search is constructed of many key elements. They include attitude, perseverance, goal definition, visual, oral and written self-presentation, and adequate research. In any specific situation, or at any stage in the progress of one's personal job search, one or another of these factors may be of paramount importance. Obtaining a job is rather like building a house. The nails are important. So are the boards, the sills, the cement, the bricks, the mortar, the paneling, the roofing materials, and all the other components. Most important, however, is the way in which they are utilized, how they are put together. You may find this answer unsatisfactorily long-winded. If so, let me give you a shorter answer to your question:

"The most important factor in a job search is the acceptance of the idea that it is necessary and proper to work for a living."

A well-known exemplar of this philosophy once wrote: "My father taught me to work, but not to love it. I never did like to work, and I don't deny it. I'd rather read, tell stories, crack jokes, talk, laugh—anything but work."

And yet, Abe Lincoln did manage to get quite a bit accomplished during his lifetime, didn't he?

Dear Secrets:

Recently, I became embroiled in a heated argument about résumés with my husband's sister. She is looking for work in what she terms a "male-dominated job market" and feels that including personal information such as her marital status in her résumé could lead to some form of discrimination by potential employers. I have always been told to include this information to round out the picture. Can you help us settle this dispute?

Embroiled

Dear Embroiled:

I hate to take sides in a family disagreement but your sister-in-law has a valid point. The information involved here is your own and you are well advised to use it sparingly. Your height, the state of your health, the number of children you have, and other personal data are out of place in a résumé. Why provide information which no one has requested and which could work to your detriment? There will be time enough to round out the picture and discuss personal topics later on.

What should be included, however, is a one-line entry indicating your hobbies or interests. Three or four items will suffice. Often this material can be used by an interviewer to "break the ice," that is, to begin an informal chat with you before getting down to the nitty gritty topics that relate directly to the job in question.

Dear Secrets:

I am completely fed up with my present position and have definitely made up my mind to change jobs. I am even considering changing careers but the question is: How can I know what's available, what's "out there"? I'd like to be really sure that I have explored all the possibilities before making a commitment to a new field. As you can imagine, I'd rather not go through all this every couple of years.

Explorer

Dear Explorer:

Even if you do have to go through it all again, don't despair. People change careers on an average of three to five times in a lifetime. But, congratulations! By all means look closely before you leap. You are proceeding methodically and your timing is right.

Unfortunately, there is no such thing as a job market in the sense of a meeting place where employers and employees gather to display their wares. I have a hunch, though, that you have been diligently studying the classified ads for some time, and that this is contributing to your sense of frustration. And well it might! Only about 6% of all jobs ever hit the papers. Scan the help-wanted section on a daily basis but don't spend more than a half an hour or so. Move on to more productive approaches.

Fully 85% of all jobs are never made public. You have to ferret them out. How? Well, why not start at the library and peruse the reference works they can put at your disposal: *The Thomas Register* for company profiles; *Moody's Industrial Register* to find out what businesses do; *McRae's Blue Book*, to name only a few. Reference librarians are there to help you. Some libraries even have special career development sections.

If you are unsure of how you would like to spend those 40 working hours each week, take a look at the *Dictionary of Occupational Titles* to see what people are doing for a living in our society. It will give you some very good ideas as to where your niche might be, and it will definitely broaden your understanding of the world we live in.

Bibliography

SELF-ASSESSMENT

Brownstone, David M. and Hawes, Gene R. *The Complete Career Guide.* New York: Simon and Schuster, 1980.

Haldane, Bernard. *Career Satisfaction and Success: A Guide to Job Freedom.* New York: AMACON Executive Books, 1978.

_____. *Career Satisfaction and Success: How to Know and Manage Your Strengths* (revised edition). New York: AMACON Executive Books, 1982.

Hawes, Gene R. *The Encyclopedia of Second Careers.* New York: Facts on File, 1984.

Molloy, John. *Dress for Success.* New York: Warner Books, 1975.

RESUME PREPARATION

Biegeleisen, Jacob I. *Job Résumés.* New York: Putnam Publishing Group, 1976.

Bostwick, Burdette. *Résumé Writing: A Comprehensive How-to-Do-It Guide.* New York: Catalyst, 1980.

Jackson, Tom. *The Perfect Résumé.* New York: Doubleday, 1981.

Reed, Jean, (Ed.). *Résumés That Get Jobs.* New York: Arco, 1981.

Résumé Preparation Manual. New York: Catalyst, 1980.

THE INTERVIEW

Bostwick, Burdette E. *One Hundred Eleven Proven Techniques and Strategies for Getting the Job.* New York: Wiley, 1983.

Crystal, John C. and Bolles, Richard N. *Where Do I Go from Here with My Life?* Berkeley: Ten Speed Press, 1980.

Metley, Anthony H. *Sweaty Palms: The Neglected Art of Being Interviewed*. Berkeley: Ten Speed Press, 1984.

Sitzman, Marion and Garcia, Leroy. *Successful Interviewing*. Lincolnwood IL: National Textbook, 1983.

JOB SEARCH

Azrin, Nathan, and Victoria B. Besalel. *Finding a Job*. Berkeley: Ten Speed Press, 1982.

Bolles, Richard. *What Color is Your Parachute?* Berkeley: Ten Speed Press, 1984.

Haldane, Bernard. *The Young People's Job Finding Guide: Job Power*. Washington: Acropolis, 1982.

Jackson, Tom and Mayleas Davidyne. *The Hidden Job Market for the Eighties*. New York: Time Books, 1981.

Jackson, Tom. *Guerilla Tactics in the Job Market*. New York: Bantam, 1978.

_____. *How to Get the Job You Want in Twenty Eight Days*. New York: Dutton, 1982.

Lathrop, Richard. *Who's Hiring Who*. Berkeley: Ten Speed Press, 1977.

Lee, Rose P. *A Real Job for You: An Employment Guide for Teens*. White Hall: Betterway Publications, 1985.

Rogers, Bob, Steve Johnson, and Jack Crawford. *The New Mosaic: Job Clubs*. Albany: Beeline Books, 1985.

Russo, Jo Ann. *Careers Without College: No B.S. Necessary*. White Hall: Betterway Publications, 1986.

Smith, Demaris C. *Temporary Employment: The Flexible Alternative*. White Hall: Betterway Publications, 1985.

Glossary

Blind Ad — A brief entry in the help-wanted section of a newspaper, consisting of a brief job description and a post office box number for résumés. Such ads are frequently used by companies which are planning to enter a new geographical area and wish to assess the feasibility of such a venture. Since blind ads often do not constitute a real offer of employment, the chances are very high that no response will be forthcoming.

Cognitive Process — A very important concept when it comes to interview preparation and performance. Individuals should research employers prior to appearing in person and should make an effort to bear in mind both the employer's needs and their own qualifications while the interview is in progress. We discourage you from practicing rote responses. Staying alert to what is going on is the key to a successful interview.

"Who Do You Know" List — A list of friends, acquaintances and other social contacts to be developed by jobseekers for use in conjunction with the networking concept.

Game Playing — A concept originally developed by Eric Berne to describe certain behavior patterns. This is perhaps the most unproductive way to deal with the difficulties of getting a job and requires a careful self-examination.

Goals — The importance of setting goals cannot be over-emphasized. This is an essential first step in any job search because it supplies the direction in which all energies will be channeled. However, a person's goals may be reset and adjusted as a job search progresses.

Hidden Job Market — A term designating the approximately 85% of all job openings which are never made public and are therefore not accessible through traditional channels.

Job Information Center — The section of a library dealing with employment matters: State and Federal civil service job listings, job service microfiche viewer, books, pamphlets, etc.

JTPA (Job Training Partnership Act) — A federally funded program created to replace CETA. Whereas CETA stressed public service employment and provided income maintenance stipends for schooling and training programs, JTPA emphasizes placement in the private sector and provides only minimal payments based on the need for lunch money, bus tokens, etc.

Networking — The skill of expanding personal contacts to reach people who do hiring, who know someone who does, or who are otherwise in a position to provide valuable leads or information.

On-the-Job Training Program — An incentive program providing employers of qualified individuals with a salary reimbursement of up to 50% during specified training periods.

References — Every jobseeker should be equipped with at least three references before going out on interviews. It is essential: a) that all references have been contacted by the jobseeker and informed that they will be used as references, and b) that these individuals can be reached by telephone during business hours for this purpose.

Résumé, Chronological — A résumé listing positions held starting with the present job and working back in time. More precisely termed a "reverse chronological" résumé.

Résumé, Functional — A résumé formatted in such a way as to stress skills, capabilities and experience while de-emphasizing dates, job titles and employers.

Self Assessment (Career) — The identification of skills and experience in each individual jobseeker. The first step in a thorough job search is to clarify goals and arrive at a realistic view of your own potential.

Statistical Trap — A pitfall involving the use of unemployment statistics to justify being out of work as opposed to developing a positive, goal-oriented job-search strategy.

Targeted Jobs Tax Credits — A tax advantage given to employers of individuals falling within certain specified categories (ex-offenders, economically disadvantaged individuals, Vietnam-era veterans). Detailed information is available through State Employment Agencies.

The Direct (or Telephone) Approach — The telephone approach is of the utmost importance in getting work. Calling potential employers for interviews and thereby establishing direct contact is one of the most productive job-search strategies.

Thank-you Notes — An extremely high percentage of jobseekers do not realize that every interview—even a negative one—should be followed up with a thank-you note. The job market is in a constant state of flux. An employer who says "no" today could easily be looking for an employee a week from now. The person who sends a thank-you note stands a better chance for employment in the future because the employer will remember him.

Traditional Approaches to Job Seeking — Entails using classified newspaper ads, school and college placement offices, state and private employment agencies. Heavily overused by most jobseekers, it accounts for only 15% of all employment obtained.

Unemployment Syndrome — A vicious cycle among the unemployed which consists of failure to find work and the resulting dejection and despair. This, in turn, undermines jobseekers' self-confidence and renders them less effective in achieving their employment goals.

Appendix

FUNCTIONAL RESUME

JOSEPHINE KEYES
12 MAIN STREET
ALBANY, NY 12222
(581) 889-6666

BACKGROUND   Experienced in several related occupational areas (Personnel Management, Employment Counseling, Teaching, Recruitment) which require excellent organizational, human relation, and communication skills.

PROFESSIONAL EXPERIENCE

Personnel
Management

* Developed and wrote personnel policy for employment communications corporation.
* Researched and instituted health plan for professional staff.
* Established, maintained, and updated personnel file system; interviewed and evaluated all staff members.
* Instituted periodic staff evaluation and performance procedures.

Employment
Counselling

* Facilitated intensive and successful group job-search program with informational, motivational and practical components.
* Counseled individual clients on job search strategies and employability readiness.
* Conducted workshops for resume preparation and interviewing techniques.

EMPLOYMENT

1982-Present   City of Albany School District, Department of Human Resources, Albany, NY

1983-1984   Sage Associates, 169 Central Ave., Albany, NY

1979-1982   New York State Assembly, Albany, NY

EDUCATION   B.A. - 1981
State University of New York at Albany

REFERENCES WILL BE FURNISHED UPON REQUEST

CHRONOLOGICAL RESUME

CARL P. DENTON
2411 Crandall Boulevard
Madison, Wisconsin 34337
(608) 422-8334

CAREER GOAL: A career in Building Maintenance with a company which offers opportunity for advancement.

WORK HISTORY

7/85 - 8/86   CARPENTER/MAINTENANCE WORKER
               Self-employed, Albany, New York

               Performed building maintenance including painting, window repair, carpet and linoleum replacement, building of camp, and structural additions to camp.

12/83 - 7/85   MAINTENANCE WORKER
               Hi-Quality Installation, St. Petersburg, Florida

               Handled all aspects of building maintenance including plumbing, electrical work, interior alterations.

6/83 - 11/83   CARPENTER
               Howe Home Construction, St. Albans, Vermont

               Built houses from ground level; framed and roofed.

7/82 - 6/83   CARPENTER
               Alcort Enterprises, Oneonta, New York

               Built houses, framed and roofed.

RELATED INFORMATION: I possess all necessary tools.

EDUCATION   Two-year Certificate in Carpentry
               Suffolk County Occupational Center

               Course included use and care of tools, principles of construction, building materials, reading plans and blueprints, terminology.

               Roosevelt Memorial High School - 1982

RELATED   Plumbing, Electrical Work, Installation of doors and
SKILLS   windows, Masonry, Roofing, Siding, Rough and some Finish Carpentry.

HOBBIES   Swimming, Fishing, Hunting, Sketching, Skating

               REFERENCES WILL BE PROVIDED UPON REQUEST

CHRONOLOGICAL RESUME - "BEFORE"

PROFESSIONAL OBJECTIVE: TO SEEK A CHALLENGING POSITION WITH A
PROMINENT COMPANY AS A COMPUTER OPERATOR.

EDUCATION: 12/84 - 6/85 AMEREX BUSINESS SCHOOL, PLAIN, MI.
CURRICULUM FOR COMPUTER OPERATIONS:

INTRODUCTION TO DATA PROCESS	100 HRS
ACCOUNTING	120 HRS
OPERATIONS LAB #1	60 HRS
PROGRAMMING BASIC II	120 HRS
OPERATIONS LAB #1	60 HRS
SYSTEMS ANALYSIS & DESIGN	140 HRS
TOTAL CLOCK HOURS	600 HRS

9/80 - 6/84 CENTRAL SCHOOL, PLAIN, MI
CURRICULUM: COLLEGE ENTRANCE DIPLOMA: REGENTS

SKILLS: EXPERIENCE WITH: IBM 3276 COMPUTER SYSTEM
IBM 3262 PRINTER
IBM 3742 KEY TO DISK MACHINE
IBM 26 KEYPUNCH MACHINE
WANG VS, 128K, COMPUTER SYSTEM
PROGRAMMING IN BASIC II
TYPING 50 WPM BOOKKEEPING

WORK EXPERIENCE:
7/85 - PRESENT: D & A WIRE AND CABLE
100 GLASS ST.   SUPERVISOR: ED JOYCE
BRAD, MI 12222
COMPUTER OPERATOR
DUTIES:
1. BILLING ON CRT
2. SALES ORDER ENTRY ON CRT
3. ACCOUNTS PAYABLE
4. ACCOUNTS RECEIVABLE

9/84 - 11/84 N.Y.S. MEDICAL ASSOCIATION
90 SWAN   SUPERVISOR: DORMAN PETERS
ST. ALBANS, NY.
SECRETARY
DUTIES:
1. RESPONSIBLE FOR BLUE CROSS/BLUE SHIELD BILLING
2. RESPONSIBLE FOR PROCESSING OF BLUE CROSS/BLUE
SHIELD PAYMENTS
3. TYPING REPORTS, LETTERS, AND MEMOS

SUMMER 84 U.S. CENSUS BUREAU
ST. ALBANS DIVISION   SUPERVISOR: MCGRATH HOWARD
ENUMERATOR
DUTIES:
1. RECORDING DATA
2. CODING DATA FOR COMPUTER INPUT
3. CONDUCTING INTERVIEWS

PERSONAL
INFORMATION: ADDRESS: BOX 18   HEIGHT: 5'6"
PLAIN, MI 12040   WEIGHT: 125 LBS.
(555) 656-6666   HEALTH: EXCELLENT
MARITAL STATUS: SINGLE

CHRONOLOGICAL RESUME - "AFTER"

John Henry Brown
Box 18
Plain, Michigan 12040
(555) 656-6666

PROFESSIONAL OBJECTIVE	A responsible position in Computer Operations with opportunity for advancement.

WORK EXPERIENCE

7/85 - Present

COMPUTER OPERATOR
D & A Wire and Cable, 100 Glass Street, Brad, MI

Handles accounts payable and accounts receivable. Enters orders and billing on CRT. Also in charge of telephone collections.

9/84 - 11/84

SECRETARY
NYS Medical Association, 90 Swan St., Albany, NY

Processed Blue Cross and Blue Shield billing and payments. Typed letters, reports, and memos.

Summer 1984

ENUMERATOR
U.S. Census Bureau, Albany District, Albany, NY

Conducted interviews, recorded and coded data for computer input.

SKILLS

Bookkeeping, Typing (50 wpm), Experienced with IBM 3276 Computer System, IBM 32632 Printer, IBM 3743 Key to Disk, IBM 26 Key punch, Wang VS 128K, Computer System Programming in Basic II and 10 Key operation.

EDUCATION

Amerex Business School, Plain, Michigan - 1981

Introductory Data Processing, Accounting, Operations, Programming, Systems Analysis and Design.

Central School, Plain, Michigan - 1984

Regents Diploma

HOBBIES

Photography, Sports, Horseback Riding

REFERENCES

Will be furnished upon request

SAMPLE LETTER OF RECOMMENDATION

Sedge Associates
416 Morton Avenue
Yonkers, N.Y. 12103
June 1, 1986

To Whom It May Concern:

This letter is to advise you that I have known Lisa Lassiter for more than five years and during that period of time I have found her to be a pleasant, trustworthy, loyal and dedicated member of society.

I recommend her highly and sincerely feel that she would be an asset to any organization.

Yours truly,

R.J. Bill
President

<u>**RESPONSE TO AN AD - SAMPLE COVER LETTER**</u>

142 State St.
Albany, N.Y. 12206
July 23, 1986

Mr. Albert D. Glisson, Manager
Parts Department
Sturgess Dodge and Honda, Inc.
1333 Central Ave.
Albany, N.Y. 12203

Dear Mr. Glisson:

I am writing in response to the advertisement in today's <u>Times Union</u> for an auto parts person. For the past three years, while taking a high school automotive mechanics course, I have worked after school in my uncle's garage. While there, I became familiar with the names and purposes of most automotive parts.

I have also made out bills for my uncle and feel sure that I could handle the recordkeeping involved.

My resume is enclosed and I can be contacted anytime at the number listed. I look forward to meeting you and discussing the position as soon as possible.

Yours truly,

Lisa Lassiter

SAMPLE INTERVIEW THANK YOU NOTE

25 Meadowland St.
Albany, N.Y. 12206
July 25, 1986

Mr. William Bradshaw
Ace Trucking Co.
1388 State St.
Albany, N.Y. 12201

Dear Mr. Bradshaw:

I just wanted to express my thanks and tell you how much I enjoyed the conversation today. The bookkeeping job sounds very interesting.

I believe my skills and experience really qualify me for this job. One thing I neglected to mention during the interview is that I maintain the books for my local Girl Scout group and have done so for the past three years.

Again, thank you for your time. I am looking forward to hearing from you about your decision.

Sincerely,

Lisa Lassiter

REFERRED BY - A SAMPLE NETWORKING LETTER

> 25 Meadowland St.
> Albany, N.Y. 12206
> July 25, 1986

Mr. Howard Jessup
Brendan, Returd and Carey
488 Broadway
Albany, N.Y. 12205

Dear Mr. Jessup:

Recently I had the good fortune to be interviewed for a job by
Mr. Albert D. Glisson of Sturgess, Dodge and Honda, Inc. At the
time, Mr. Glisson felt that my qualifications were more than sufficient
for the advertised position and suggested that I contact you.

I have enclosed my resume, and, as it indicates, I have had excellent
training with the NCR Bookkeeping system.

May I call you and get your advice? A few minutes of your time is all
I ask. If I do not hear from you by February 7, I shall call you.

> Yours truly,

> Lisa Lassiter

Index